Challenge to the Church

CHALLENGE TO THE CHURCH

The case of Archbishop Lefebvre

YVES CONGAR OP

Preface by George Patrick Dwyer,
Archbishop of Birmingham

OUR SUNDAY VISITOR, INC.
HUNTINGDON, INDIANA

This English translation by Paul Inwood
© 1976 William Collins Sons & Co Ltd
First published as *La crise dans l'Englise et Mgr Lefebvre*
© Les Editions du Cerf 1976

This edition was published by arrangement
with William Collins Sons & Co. Ltd.

ISBN 0-87973-689-5
Library of Congress Catalog Card Number: 76-53715

Published in the U.S.A. by
Our Sunday Visitor, Inc.
Noll Plaza
Huntingdon, Indiana 46750

689

Made and printed in Great Britain

Contents

Preface by *George Patrick Dwyer,*
Archbishop of Birmingham   6

To the Reader by *Yves M.-J. Congar OP*   8

1 What Mgr Lefebvre refuses to accept   11

2 An evaluation of the Council   37

3 The present crisis   50

4 Towards a solution   66

APPENDICES
  I. Mgr Lefebvre's 'Profession of Faith'   77
 II. Handwritten letters from Paul VI   79
III. The future of the Council by *Jean Guitton*   82
IV. Action Francaise and Action Catholique:
    a brief explanation by *Francis Whyte*   88

Footnotes   91

Preface

There has never been a General Council of the Church which has not been followed by a crisis of Faith for some part of the people, and even by a schism. The present sad events connected with Archbishop Lefebvre and Ecône follow a historical pattern. But General Councils are summoned to deal with crises, they are not the cause of them. Those who attribute the present crisis to Vatican II were reasonably answered by one who said that if the Council had not been held the crisis now would be much worse. It was already there before the Council. Pius XII was aware of it. Father Congar who writes this little book was aware of it, was involved in it, and lived it through with unflinching loyalty to the Church.

He writes now to offer guidance to what is happening and to find a solution to the troubles. These pages are illumined by a sense of history and a deep love of the Church – two things which are above all necessary today. They show clarity and patience allied to theological and spiritual discernment.

Archbishop Lefebvre stands for a rigid conservatism which seems to have no place for the necessary development which the Council had to undertake to meet the problems of a world in ferment. Father Congar understands the mentality – not least because he is a Frenchman and this is a very French style of quarrel. (Maybe it is a vindication of Belloc's dictum that for centuries all the great questions affecting the Faith and Western civilization have been fought out in France).

6

Certainly this is not simply a question of liturgical rites. The point at issue is fidelity to the Council and the 'mind of the Church'. Therefore Father Congar also offers an examination of conscience not only to the ultra-conservatives but to all of us, and not least to those who have gone to the other extreme of liturgical and doctrinal 'go as you please'.

There is sympathy and real affection in this booklet for all who are suffering the 'post-operation' pains of Vatican II. To understand and indeed to share that suffering is the first step to reconciliation.

✠ *George Patrick Dwyer*
Archbishop of Birmingham

To the Reader

The only reason I have written this little book is love of the Church and love of the unity of her communion. By force of circumstances it has become more critical, if not more negative, than I would have liked. This is the price that I have paid for taking seriously the rejections of Mgr Lefebvre and his disciples, the repercussions of whose doings and thoughts have filled the Press and radio for two months now.

As far as I am concerned, the seminarians of Ecône, and the faithful in the Salle Wagram or the sports stadium at Lille, are brothers – but brothers who are mistaken about the Council and the eucharistic liturgy promulgated by Paul VI. The following pages are offered to them for reflection and, should the occasion arise, to promote a discussion which I would not refuse to take part in. What they are reproached with has nothing to do with holding on to the Catholic faith or wanting a sacred dignity in priests whose formation is sober and rigorous. They are reproached with rejecting, as if stained with error, an ecumenical Council and reforms which have been brought to fruition in all seriousness, approved by the supreme authority, and received and implemented in the Catholic Church as a whole. How can they talk about 'bastard sacraments' when they are received by millions of Catholics every day, or refer to 'bastard priests'-meaning us who celebrate these sacraments? That doesn't make sense.

This stage would not have been reached, say many of the faithful who accept the Council and the present reforms, had not so many anarchical innovations, so many aberrant proposals, such rash abandonment proliferated since the Council without any decisive reaction from the responsible authorities. But let's not act as if it was always the others who are at fault. I'm at fault too. We're all involved in the drama, whether we like it or not. It's certainly not with a light heart that Mgr Lefebvre is setting himself up against the Pope. It's certainly not in a spirit of flippancy that I am criticizing him. He professes to act from love of truth and the Church. So do I.

It would be impossible to say everything, to deal with all the questions, to answer all the criticisms and doubts. Dear Reader, please don't be annoyed with me. Open the pages of this little book and read it right through to the end in the spirit in which it was written: it only aims to help brother-Catholics to set themselves on their feet (again) or to remain lucidly in the full and joyous communion of the Church that is one, holy, catholic and apostolic, the Church of today, the eternal Church.

In the service and glory of our God who is Father, Son and Holy Spirit.

3 September 1976   *Yves M.-J. Congar OP*
on the feast of
St Gregory the Great

Note

Since the drafting of this book – in fact since its setting-up in type – we have learnt that the Holy Father received Mgr Lefebvre at Castelgandolfo on 11 September 1976. For me, and for all concerned with peace in true light, this is a great joy and a real hope. I thought for a moment of stopping the publication of this booklet, but the tone of it, which reflects the spirit in which it was written, isn't unfriendly. The questions asked in it are real questions, and are being asked in the terms which I have used. Many are still asking them and will still be asking them tomorrow. I am therefore allowing this little book to see the light of day, without changing a single word of it; and I fill it with an even greater love for the Church, her unity, and all her faithful servants.

14 September 1976   Y.C.

1. What Mgr Lefebvre refuses to accept

What is at stake, and the implications

Ecône and Mgr Lefebvre again? Aren't the burning questions the Church is faced with throughout the whole wide world far more important? Even if I know nothing about such things, how can these issues divert attention from the Gospel-based work which is springing up all over the place; voluntary catechists, prayer-groups, so much help given in so many cases of distress? How can I accept the fact that the fuss over one instance of disobedience is obscuring the faithful, daily work of tens of thousands of layfolk, priests and nuns who, without broadcasting the fact, are ensuring that the Church lives in the thick of an overpowering, problematical world?

Ecône is not of lesser importance than all this. It is important because of the young people there who are preparing to serve the Lord Jesus in the priesthood; because of the injury done to the peace of the Church by the turn which events have taken since the spring of 1974; and because the 'Ecône drama', transmitted and sometimes blown up out of all proportion by the mass media, has as it were revealed a dissatisfaction and an uneasiness felt by many of the faithful. The opinion-polls are worth what they're worth – nothing more. What results would you get from an opinion-poll on the installation of a nuclear power-station near a large town, if the poll were conducted the day after an accident had taken place? And again, what would the results be if the poll took place during the summer holidays when television and radio stations and the newspapers have empty space to fill? The opinion-poll carried out by the IFOP [the French national opinion-poll organization] and published on 13 August 1976 in the newspaper *Le Progrès de Lyon* was doubtless able to profit from a particular conjunction of events. But that doesn't make it any less significant. According to the poll, twenty-eight per cent of Catholics approve of the attitudes of Mgr Lefebvre and forty-eight per cent of practising Catholics think that the Church has gone too far.

These are very vague indications. 'Too far' on what point? 'Too far' from what? To what extent? 'The attitudes of Mgr Lefebvre'; which ones? His action in the 'traditional' formation of priests? His rejection of the Council? They are not the same thing. The figures too need to be checked. I prefer the appraisal of the situation by J. Gritti, a good religious sociologist, in his reply to that excellent journalist, Jean-Claude Petit:

A schism is fuelled by people who, little by little, latch themselves on to the notorious doings of the opposition. Let's say that there could be a few tens of thousands of people at the most. The other side of the coin is that many traditional Christians who have suffered – for example, because of the liturgical reforms – and who have nevertheless remained faithful to their community, are going to suffer again because of what is happening; but they will accept the position of the Pope and the bishops. I would therefore say that, beside the 2% who may break away, there are 15% who feel 'lost' to varying extents, without wanting to give a pejorative meaning to the word. (*La Vie Catholique* no. 1616, 18–23 August 1976, p. 14)

What exactly is at stake? As loyally and as clearly as we can, we would like to tell our brothers in the faith.

REJECTION OF THE COUNCIL
AND WHAT FOLLOWED IT

What's it all about? That's the question that Foch always used to ask.

What is at issue is not the use of Latin, nor the wearing of the clerical cassock, nor the regime of life at the seminary of Ecône. This regime is just like the one I followed with so many other students at the Seminary des Carmes from 1921 to 1924 – years which were prayerful and happy. What is at issue is the acceptance of the Second Vatican Council, and its sixteen documents, signed by the whole of the Catholic episocpacy, and approved and promulgated by the Holy Father; and then the acceptance of reforms – particularly the liturgical ones – which were undertaken by the Council, formulated in Rome or worked out in detail by the pastoral authorities of each country, and approved by the Pope. Such an acceptance is necessary in order to live fully, effectively and concretely in the Church's communion *today*.

Mgr Lefebvre and his followers – but certainly not the twenty-eight per cent of Catholics who say that they approve of his actions – declare that:

We adhere wholeheartedly and with our whole soul to Catholic Rome, Guardian of the Catholic Faith and of the traditions necessary to maintain that Faith, to Eternal Rome, Mistress of Wisdom and of Truth.

On the other hand we refuse and have always refused to follow the Rome of neo-modernist and neo-Protestant tendencies which clearly manifested themselves in the Second Vatican Council and after the Council in all the reforms which issued from it. (. . .)

This reform, the fruit of liberalism and modernism, is completely and utterly poisoned. (. . .) It is accordingly impossible for any aware and faithful Catholic to adopt this reform and to submit to it any way whatever.

For our salvation, the sole attitude of fidelity to the Church and to Catholic doctrine is the categorical refusal of acceptance of the reform.[1]

This is a rejection of the Council. It is a declaration of adherence to 'Rome'. It is surprising to learn that Mgr Lefebvre has obstinately refused the act of submission which the Holy Father asked of him not only through the intermediary efforts of bishops and cardinals but by a first personal letter of 29 June 1975, a second handwritten letter of 8 September 1975, and a third of 15 August 1976, not to mention pressing, fraternal, even affectionate exhortations. Mgr Lefebvre himself, in addressing Paul VI, has used formulae like 'my profound submission to the successor of Peter which I renew in placing my hands between the hands of Your Holiness'. That is to say that he makes a distinction between what is expressed as 'Eternal Rome' or what is involved in the succession of Peter in Paul VI, and what in the actions of present-day Rome and Paul VI is spiced, in his opinion, with abhorrent liberalism or modernism. As far as he is concerned, he is the one to judge what is admissible and what is heretical or false and therefore to be rejected by fidelity to 'the Church as she has always been'. One thing is certain: neither Pius XII, nor Pius XI, nor Pius X, nor Pius IX, nor Pius V, the popes to whom Mgr Lefebvre is always referring, would have admitted such a distinction.

Mgr Lefebvre has, several times over, spelt out what above all he rejects and why. He is especially concerned with three themes of the Council in which he sees an ecclesiastical application of the principles of the French Revolution of 1789: liberty, equality, fraternity.

On the subject of the Council's *Declaration on Religious Liberty*, he has said:

> Religious liberty corresponds to the term 'liberty' in the French Revolution; it is an analogous term which the devil willingly makes use of.

On the subject of the collegiality of bishops:

> Collegiality is the destruction of personal authority. Democracy is the destruction of God's authority, the Pope's authority, Bishops' authority. Collegiality corresponds to the equality of the 1789 Revolution.

On the subject of the *Decree on Ecumenism* and the *Declaration on Non-Christian Religions*:

> If you pay attention, you will see that this corresponds to 'fraternity'. Heretics have been described as brothers, Protestants have been called 'separated brothers'. There's your fraternity. Yes, we're well off with ecumenism; it's fraternity with the communists.[2]

FOUNDED ON POLITICAL INSPIRATION?

What we call integrism or, more generally, opposition

to the open-and-above-board, still has a conservative
and anti-democratic background *in France*.* The first
edition of my book *Vraie et fausse réforme dans l'Eglise*
(*True and false reform in the Church*) in 1950 contained, on
pages 604–22, an Appendix on the 'Mentality of "the
Right" and integrism'. I suppressed this in the 1969
reprint as a peaceful gesture towards the integrists.[3]
However, much of my historical data and analysis still
remains true. What we know of the formation of Mgr
Lefebvre[4], what we have learnt about his conduct in
Dakar[5], what we have heard about him and know of
him at the Council[6], his declarations since then, the
uniform spirit running through his writings and his
actions – all these things proclaim him to be a man of
the Right, in agreement with the attitudes of the old
Action Française. Here we have a set of characteristic
attitudes and procedures: sticking disparaging labels
on one's opponents, while never admitting that one
might be in error oneself[7]; gathering everything that
one detests under an umbrella term which arouses
unqualified emotional repulsion[8]; insisting that one is
right, while sometimes displaying a pettifogging spirit
in so doing; being convinced that there is a wicked plot,
that a 'Judaeo-Masonic' or communist conspiracy has
infiltrated the Church, is working inside it, and is
fomenting internal subversion.[9]

Not all Mgr Lefebvre's sympathisers exhibit all these
characteristics, and not all to the same extent. He
himself is too much a man of the Church, too much a
master of himself and, moreover, too nice to be political
and sectarian to this extent, though his speech on 29
August 1976 at Lille, from which we will be quoting
later, does provoke anxiety. Others who are opposed to

* For a brief description of the political environment to which
the author is referring, see Appendix IV [Translator's note].

the Council's reforms or to Paul VI are very 'Action Française': Jean Madiran and Georges de Nantes (who does not, by the way, agree with Mgr Lefebvre). Without going so far as an explicitly anti-democratic political position, more or less formal opposition to the reforms issuing from the Council, and critical reservations regarding the present direction of the Church both originate in a conservative ethos and a defensive reflex against change in general: in the midst of so many upsets or baffling innovations the Church at least should remain fixed, stable and secure. A flag-officer said to Mgr Weber, Bishop of Strasburg, as he was leaving for the Council: 'Above all, let nothing be changed!' But there we have an enormous problem, that is *the* problem which exists now. We will come back to it later.

A Catholic may certainly be opposed to democracy as a political regime, provided he uses his intelligence in adopting this position. He may be 'of the Right' with the same proviso, and also on condition that he is prepared to let a living sense of the Church and a lively sense of the Gospel govern his group reflexes. At least three of my friends are well able to maintain this balance. I am not, therefore, taking issue at a political level. I ask only that a person should be clear about himself, intelligently critical concerning his conditioning; and I ask this from the point of view of an ideology which mingles with our most strongly-held beliefs – that in the final analysis we should allow the Gospel a transcendence and a freedom of which the Lord Jesus is forever the example and the source.

Witnesses who attended the Mass on 29 August 1976 at the sports stadium in Lille, together with the six daily newspapers and the two weeklies that I read, are unanimous in stating that this event had a strongly-marked political flavour; news-sheets sold at the gates, regimentation, Mgr Lefebvre's speech, rounds of applause – all were significant. *Le Monde* used the headline 'The mask has been thrown aside'. What was revealed had been fairly clear to me for a long time. However, I wouldn't want this to divert me from recognizing the serious questions which are being posed *about the Church*, nor those which are being put *to the Church*.

REJECTING THE COUNCIL MEANS PUTTING ONESELF ON THE FRINGE OF THE CATHOLIC CHURCH AND REJECTING THE AUTHORITY OF THE POPE

Vatican II wasn't perfect, in the eyes either of the 'conservative' elements or of the 'progressive' elements; but, more than any other ecumenical council in history, it had all the guarantees of authenticity. Like no other, it brought the whole Church together in the person of its pastors. It was far more heedful of its minority which was conservative, than Vatican I had been. I can personally vouch for this from the different commissions on which I worked. The Theological Commission owed the quality of its work and the balance of its texts in part to the tenacity of its minority group. The Holy Father did everything he could, even going so far as to run the risk of unpopularity, to create conditions in which the anxieties of the minority would be calmed and the final vote of the assembly would be as nearly unanimous as possible. Thus, for instance, the *Nota praevia* to chapter III of the *Dogmatic Constitution on the Church* or the nineteen last-minute *modi* (amendments) to the *Decree on Ecumenism*.

In fact the texts received a definitive *placet* from

such a majority of the Council Fathers that the results were almost unanimous. A Vatican spokesman revealed on 27 August 1976 that Mgr Lefebvre himself had signed nearly every one of the Council texts, in particular those on the liturgy and ecumenism. Here are the voting figures for the documents some of whose conclusions are disputed by some of the integrists:

The Constitution *Sacrosanctum Concilium, On the liturgy*: 2,158 for, 19 against.

The Dogmatic Constitution *Lumen gentium, On the Church*: 2,151 for, 5 against.

The Decree *Unitatis redintegratio, On Ecumenism*: 2,137 for, 11 against.

The Pastoral Constitution *Gaudium et spes, On the Church in the Modern World*: 2,309 for, 75 against.

The Declaration *Dignitatis humanae personae, On Religious Liberty*: 2,308 for, 70 against.

The Declaration *Nostra aetate, On Non-Christian Religions*: 2,221 for, 88 against.

With regard to the last of these, it must be especially noted that negative votes could have been motivated by very different – and even opposing – reasons: for example, over-favourable/unfavourable to the Jews. It's also worth noting that even at the Council of Nicea, attended by 250 bishops, there were two negative votes. At Vatican I, seventy minority bishops left Rome on the eve of the final vote so that they would not have to say *Non placet*; the result of the vote on 18 July 1870 was 533 for, 2 against. When a conciliar text is voted upon, and then approved and promulgated by the Pope, it becomes normative for the Church, the kind of 'normativity' depending on the character of the document; formal dogma (Vatican II didn't produce any), common doctrine, simple law. . . . Catholics, headed by the bishops, must subscribe to the ecclesial consensus which is thereafter 'in possession'. That doesn't prevent either research or discussion on matters which are still open to argument, but it does determine certain exigencies in the Catholic communion.

It is one thing to discuss one point or another which has actually been left open for discussion; it is quite another thing to profess (and to act in consequence of that profession) that

'We refuse to follow the Rome of neo-modernist and neo-Protestant tendencies which clearly manifested themselves in the Second Vatican Council and after the Council in all the reforms which issued from it. . . . It is impossible for any conscious and faithful Catholic to adopt this reform and to submit to it in any way whatever' (Mgr Lefebvre's *Profession of Faith*, 21 August 1974).

On his return from the First Vatican Council, the Archbishop of Munich held a meeting with all the professors of his theology faculty and invited them to work for the holy Church. One of them, Döllinger, drily replied: 'Yes, for the *old* Church.' 'There is only one Church,' replied the Archbishop; 'there isn't a new one or an old one'. 'A new one has been *created*,' retorted Döllinger. The knowledgeable historian was wasting his time when, subsequently, he refused to call himself an 'Old Catholic'; he wanted to be described only as an excommunicated Catholic, but he is reckoned today among the initiators of that schism which gave rise to the Old Catholicism which is still with us.

It's worth spending a moment or two on Döllinger's situation. He was a priest but he ceased celebrating Mass and the sacraments from that time onwards; however, he still liked to pray in churches. He refused to place himself under the jurisdiction of the Old Catholic bishop and advised the Minister of Public Worship not to recognize the bishop as such. He did not want a schismatic Church and, during the first meeting of Old Catholics at Munich, 22–24 September 1871, he made this declaration: 'I have spent my life studying the history of sects and splits within the Church, and I have always seen that they ended up badly. In accepting this proposal (the establishment of parishes) we are abandoning the idea of reform *within* the Church. Allow me, dear sirs, to raise my voice to point out the danger to you.'

Döllinger confined himself to the realm of ideas. He refused to accept a definition of Vatican I, and this provides objective grounds to accuse him of personal schism and heresy. But he never at any time took steps to set up another Church.

Very instructive too is a different historical case. John Wesley (1703–91) did not want to cut himself off from the Anglican Church and the year before his death he was still protesting that he was a member of it. However, he did cut himself off and did create a new community when, in 1784, he ordained Thomas Coke as Overseer for North America. It is not for nothing that questions touching on the ministry constitute the most stubborn breaking-points between disunited Churches. We mention this in order to explain, in the Ecône-Rome drama, the importance assumed by Mgr Lefebvre's ordination on 29 June 1976 of thirteen (fourteen?) priests and thirteen deacons (subdeacons?), despite the warnings, urgent steps and interdictions coming from the Pope (there had been an ordination of three priests the previous year, but not in the same circumstances). The culminating point of rupture would be reached if Mgr Lefebvre consecrated a bishop. In our opinion, this would raise questions concerning the validity of the ordination. Schism? That is a formidable and weighty word! We cannot avoid the question. But before tackling it, we must touch upon two other points; the status of this bishop and the clerics he ordains, and the rite of eucharistic celebration.

BISHOP OF WHERE?
CLERICS OF WHICH CHURCH?

Of the Catholic Church, they will say, and even 'of the Church as she has always been'. That's something, certainly, but it's not as simple as that. The Church is in fact a communion: a spiritual communion through the faith and love that the Holy Spirit, the one and the same Spirit, places in the heart of all; a communion conditioned and nourished in ways perceivable by the senses, since we are bodily creatures: the sacraments, baptism and eucharist, the Word concretely and historically given and formulated. . . . Since we are the People of God, gathered from the whole world and making our way through history – in that 'human caravan' that Count Plessis de Grenedan spoke of – this spiritual communion, in order to remain such, has concrete structures which nourish it, express it and govern it according to the planes and dimensions of real life: dimensions of place, time, events and people. These are its Canon Law (*quo sit Ecclesia Christi felix* – 'thanks to which the Church can live happy' – says an inscription at the old university of Salamanca), the Rules of its religious communities and all kinds of different regulations; geographically, its distribution into dioceses or ecclesiastical jurisdictions; the sacred liturgy whose forms and history are well-known today; in time, it is the word which the indefectable Church pronounces in response to changing circumstances and issues as they arise, and according to the resources which she has at her disposal. All this is manifested by real people who are what they are, but of whom God willingly makes use.

In this way the Catholic Church is distributed into dioceses which, under the pastoral care of a bishop who is titular of a see, each make up a local Church (we're talking here of the structures which are valid in our part of the world). Mgr Lefebvre is the former Archbishop-Bishop of Tulle (he occupied this see for seven months in 1962); such is the title given to him by the Holy Father. He has no diocese. At Ecône, the bishop is Mgr Nestor Adam, Bishop of Sion, who had the following text read out in all the churches of his diocese on 15 August 1976:

> From the religious point of view, Catholics are bound to follow the bishop of the diocese as long as the latter is united to the Sovereign Pontiff. [. . .] To remain a Catholic, it is absolutely necessary to recognize the authority of the present Pope, Paul VI, and of the Second Vatican Council.

In Canon Law, Mgr Lefebvre cannot take steps to ordain without the authorization of Bishop Adam (Canon 1008). The Ecône seminarians—who I am sure really want to consecrate themselves to the service of the Lord Jesus—could not have been canonically ordained without 'dimissory letters' from the bishops of their country of origin (Canons 955,962). These are the practical rules for good order which communion requires. Because they disobeyed these rules, these young ordained ministers and their consecrating bishop were declared 'suspended *a divinis*', which is to say that they cannot legitimately exercise the public acts of the sacred ministry: preaching and the celebration of the sacraments. The obligation upon ordinands to receive and present 'dimissory letters' is a concrete representation of a deeper obligation, which springs from the nature of the Church: that the ministry has reference to a local Church which has its *presbyterium* (its body of priests) and a bishop to preside over it. According to the doctrine and discipline of the Church today these ordinations are valid but irregular, illicit, and not in conformity with the established order.

The monstrous extreme in a conception of the episcopate and the priesthood which would completely isolate valid ordinations from the service of a local Church, and from communion with the universal Church, exists in what are known as *episcopi vagantes*, which we could translate as 'vagabond' or 'rogue' bishops. There are a lot of them (I personally have known two). A. J. Macdonald and H. R. T. Brendreth have each devoted a detailed study to them. These are men without a real diocese, more or less at the head of groups of their personal followers, who go about doing confirmations and ordinations. . . . Professor F. Heiler, who was consecrated by a Syrian Monophysite bishop, was able to ordain about a hundred and twenty pastors in Germany in this way. . . . I am not likening Mgr Lefebvre to an *episcopus vagans*. His case is quite singular; his personal beliefs and intentions are of an incontestable moral quality. He knows the canonical irregularity of his actions. He justifies himself by the sense of duty which this kind of necessity 'that knows not the law' imposes on him—a false necessity, born of a mistaken duty, for he is wrong about the Council and the Church after 1962-5. I have mentioned *episcopi vagantes* simply to illustrate, via their opposition to it, the theology of the local Church and its practical regulations.

REGARDING 'THE MASS OF ST PIUS V' ('THE TRIDENTINE MASS')

Mgr Lefebvre and his followers are not the only ones involved here. The Abbé Coache, Abbé Barbara, Mgr Ducaud-Bourget, the *Courrier de Rome* (which keeps finding an ever-increasing number of juridical quibbles) and many other people, have ridden to death the celebration of the 'Mass of St Pius V' and the rejection of the reformed eucharistic rites in the Missal published by order of Paul VI in 1969 as if these latter were heretical and even invalid. On 22 July 1976 French newspapers announced that twenty-three local associations had sworn to 'defend and maintain against all comers . . . the Holy Sacrifice of the Mass according to the perpetual rite, known as that of St Pius V'.

Against all comers – the 2,550 bishops and 400,000 priests who, every day, celebrate the Eucharist throughout the world, in communion with 'Paul our Pope', whom they mention in this celebration. That doesn't hold water.

It holds water even less in the light of the historical, theological, liturgical and canonical truth, as two Solesmes monks and Abbé André Richard have demonstrated with all the precision that one could wish for.[10] Let's go over the ground once more: the point at issue is not the use of Latin, nor the exclusion of the Roman Canon which, in its present state, dates from the end of the sixth century (St Gregory the Great). As for me, I celebrate Mass every day, saying, when its turn comes round, the Roman Canon which appears in the Missal of Pius V. Sometimes I celebrate in Latin (for example, when I participate in Rome at a session of the International Theological Commission). Latin Masses are celebrated in twenty Parisian parishes every Sunday. That isn't the point at issue, any more than is the Gregorian Chant whose retention the Holy Father has asked for, at least in monasteries – a thing which makes for our spiritual joy. The point at issue is historical, theological, canonical and of course pastoral.

Historical. To talk, as the twenty-three local associations do, about 'the Mass according to the perpetual rite, known as that of St Pius V', or, like Mgr Lefebvre in his homily on 29 June 1976, of the 'rite as it has always been', makes us think that someone does not know their history. The Eucharist instituted by Christ, which is indeed unchangeable, is being confused with its rite, which has manifold forms throughout the Catholic Churches and which has changed in the course of the centuries; there is a confusion between this rite – which is for some reason immediately identified with the Latin rite, and even with the Roman rite (for there are also the Ambrosian, Carthusian, and Mozarabic rites, etc) – and the Missal of Pius V. Not having been able to complete certain reforms itself, the Council of Trent entrusted the papacy with the task of bringing them to a conclusion and, in particular, of publishing a catechism for the use of priests (which Pius V did in 1566 – a beautiful text!), a breviary, a missal (which the same Pius V did in 1570), and a standard version of Holy Scripture (the Vulgate of Sixtus V in 1590). In the same way, the Second Vatican Council entrusted the Pope with the application of its liturgical reform, the broad outlines of which it had traced in its Constitution *Sacrosanctum Concilium, On the Liturgy* – the only

Council document, incidentally, which resulted from a preconciliar commission.

If this text has endured, and still endures, it's because it was the fruit – just like the liturgical reforms which have occurred since – of a liturgical scholarship and movement of great quality and vitality: a scholarship and a movement whose origins go back for more than a century and whose development has taken place over about sixty years.

To make out of the Missal of St Pius V a kind of Absolute, as if it was, without any possible modification, purely and simply identical to the Last Supper, is an untenable position. Saying this doesn't detract from the holiness of the text. I myself never followed it completely, since Pius V, who was a Dominican, gave permission for the retention of particular liturgies which could prove their existence for more than two hundred years previously – and one of these was the liturgy of the Order of Preachers (Dominicans).

Theological. The opponents of the new eucharistic rites justify their rejection – in which can be found a huge factor of irrational opposition to anything new, of deep feeling, and of stubbornness – with the following arguments:

The Mass of Paul VI does not express the aspect of sacrifice. 'How is it possible to waver between a Mass which is a real Sacrifice and a Mass which is, in a word, a Protestant form of worship, a meal, a communion, a breaking of bread, a supper, as Luther has already put it?'[11] To say that there is at the moment in the minds of numerous Catholics, even of priests, a weakening of the idea of eucharistic *sacrifice* is, I think, correct. But I must qualify that by stating that this does not affect the

27

Church's understanding of the actualization, in her sacramental celebration, of the unique sacrifice offered by Jesus on the cross: a biblical ('memorial'), traditional and Thomist[12] idea. It is therefore good that the faith of the Church should be recalled regarding this point, all the more so as there is no easy way of explaining it in greater detail. But it is quite incorrect to say that the new eucharistic prayers draw away from or even stifle the idea of sacrifice. The actual word appears twice during the Offertory; it is mentioned most formally in Eucharistic Prayers III and IV. As for Prayer II, this is taken almost word for word from the most ancient liturgical text known, that of the *Apostolic Tradition* of St Hippolytus (beginning of the third century). This is the same Hippolytus who, after having crossed swords with Pope Callixtus, whom he accused of being too easy-going on sinners, found himself in the company of this pontiff's successor, St Pontian, the pair of them condemned for the faith to be deported to Sardinia!

The Mass of Paul VI is Protestant. Mgr Lefebvre gave one of his publications the title *The Mass of Luther*. The opposition hasn't stopped quoting a remark of Brother Max Thurian of Taizé, who said that Protestants could celebrate according to the new Catholic rite. They take this to mean that the faith of the Church has been protestantized, without stopping to ask themselves if at least some Protestants haven't shifted their own beliefs since the sixteenth century, and haven't, insofar as one can thus describe it, catholicized them. Yet this is the most reasonable hypothesis: those who have read a book published by the same Brother Max Thurian before the Council: *L'Eucharistie, mémorial du Seigneur, sacrifice d'action de grâce et d'intercession* (The Eucharist:

memorial of the Lord, thanksgiving and mediatory sacrifice) (Delachaux et Niestle, 1959) would say it was a certainty. As for insinuating that the non-catholic observers had an equally non-catholic influence on the Roman Consilium where the elaboration of the liturgical reforms was carried out – this has been denied in the most categorical manner by all the members of the Consilium to whom I have put the question, and likewise by the Vatican Press Office on 25 February 1976 (*Documentation Catholique* No. 1701, 1 July 1976, p. 649).

That the Church has delighted Protestants by giving a greater prominence to the Word of God in her celebrations can scandalize only those who think that Catholicism and anti-protestantism are the same thing, in the same way that there once existed in Protestant circles those – though there are happily few of them left now – who identify anti-catholicism with true Christianity.

The Mass of Paul VI is democratic and, as such, is the expression of a new religion. The accusation is so outrageous that we feel constrained to set out below the way in which Mgr Lefebvre expressed it in his speech at the ordination ceremony on 29 June 1976:

It is obvious that this new rite is, if I may put it this way, of an opposing polarity, that it supposes a different conception of the Catholic religion, that it supposes a different religion. It is no longer the priest who offers the Holy Sacrifice of the Mass, it is the assembly. Now this is a complete programme. From now on it's also the assembly which will replace authority in the Church. It's the Assembly of Bishops which will replace the power of individual Bishops. It's the senate of priests which will replace the power of the Bishop in his diocese. It's weight of numbers which will give the orders from now on in the Holy Church. And all this is expressed in the Mass precisely because the assembly replaces the priest, to such an extent that now many priests no longer want to celebrate the Holy Mass if there isn't an assembly there.

Very quietly, it's the Protestant idea of the Mass which is creeping into Holy Church. And this is in accordance with the mentality of modern man, with the mentality of modernist man, completely in accordance, for it's the democratic ideal which is fundamentally the idea of modern man. That is to say that power is in the assembly, authority is vested in men, *en masse*, and not in God. [. . .] This Mass is no longer a hierarchic Mass, it's a democratic Mass. . . .

The small grain of truth to be found in this text at the level of statements (very vague ones) or fears put into words is marred by being mixed with uncritical political fervour and debatable theological interpretation. Let's leave on one side the sections which are beyond the pale and the abusive generalization which assumes that to say that the assembly, the *ecclesia*, in taking on at its own level and in its own way the responsibility for a celebration, is equivalent to denying that power comes from God. It's not a question here of 'power' but of communion and of the exercise by the faithful of their Christian existence, of their baptismal priesthood.[13] Tradition – at least that which wasn't inspired by anti-protestantism – is very solid on this point.[14] Many texts give voice to it, but most of all those of the liturgy itself. The liturgy maintains that the responsible subject of a celebration is the *ecclesia*, the structured Christian community, presided over by one of its *ordained* members. For this he has received in his ordination a new sharing in the priesthood of Jesus Christ: in the direct line of descent of the ministry and for the ministry, and not only in the line of descent of personal Christian existence (baptism); with the result that the priest is to be considered not only with reference to Christ whom he represents and whose part he plays to a certain extent on a visible and sacramental plane (*agit in persona Christi*) but with reference to the community which he gathers together and over which he presides. Mgr Lefebvre can see only the first reference. In the speech in question, he even expressed this first reference in very critical terms – but we won't dwell on these, convinced as we are that they exceed his real thoughts. Present studies, very much nurtured on the Old Testament and ancient tradition, emphasize the assembled Christian community and the *rapport* which the priest has with it as its 'president', this latter term signifying much more than a man sitting in an armchair. He is the one who gathers them together, the guide, the animator, who is qualified by a sacramental act to absolve and to consecrate.

Isn't this the doctrine of the Council of Trent: 'After celebrating the old Passover, Christ instituted a new Passover, that of his own immolation to be celebrated by the *ecclesia* under visible signs through the ministry of priests' (Session XXII: Denz.-Schön. 1741)?

From the canonical point of view. Since the matter has been disputed by means of excessive quibbling in the *Courrier de Rome*, we must affirm the validity of the publication of a new missal by Paul VI, together with the obligation, to make use of it in public celebrations starting from the date decreed by the local hierarchy.

We would refer in this connection to Dom Guy Oury's book, already mentioned. It is true that St Pius V declared, in the Brief *Quo primum tempore*, that those who celebrated according to the missal which he published would be forever free from all censure. The context makes the meaning of this clause very clear: it was aimed at people attached to previous missals who would be likely to rail against anyone following the thenceforward official rite. But Pius V also forbade anyone to change or make additions to his missal; however, several of his successors did precisely that – for example, Pius XII for the celebration of the Easter Vigil. The thing is that councils and popes do have the power to alter measures taken by their predecessors in order to respond to the needs of the time. Chancery-type formulae like 'for perpetual memory' shouldn't be urged in the face of the facts. I have several examples in front of me – of Boniface VIII, for instance – which are even more thunderous. And Clement XIV's Brief *Dominus ac Redemptor* of 21 July 1773, suppressing the Society of Jesus, intended that this measure should remain *perpetuo* (para 26). Pius VII reinstated the Society by the Bull *Sollicitudo omnium* of 7 August 1814, 'notwithstanding the Brief of Clement XIV of happy memory' (para 12). Papal power is equal for all pontiffs succeeding to the captaincy of the Church Militant.

The pastoral point of view, finally, deserves the greatest attention, for the sacraments are made for man; the liturgy is the praise of the Church, the Body of Christ united to its Head. This is why the law which guides pastors responsible for the cure of souls lends itself to pastoral adaptation for the spiritual needs of men, provided that the imprescriptible truth of Divine

Revelation, subject and norm of the faith, is respected. It is this which compelled the liturgical reform to take place, at the same time as inspirations and elements from a tradition more ancient than the Middle Ages or modern times were rediscovered. It's true that not everything in the renewed liturgy is marvellous. Many priests and communities do what they can with feeble resources and in difficult conditions. But the renewed liturgy of the Mass and the sacraments has allowed an 'active participation' of the faithful (the expression comes from St Pius X) which is incomparably better than in the former Latin rites. Televised Sunday Masses reveal living communities. I think that my position is not an isolated one. On that Sunday of 29 August, at the moment when Mgr Lefebvre was celebrating Mass in Lille according to the form of St Pius V, the TV was broadcasting a very simple Mass from a chapel in Lantic (Côtes-du-Nord). I loved the Latin Mass, which I celebrated for nearly forty years, but I wouldn't want to go back to it. I recently assisted (and, as a priest, concelebrated) at a 'St Pius V' Mass on the occasion of the burial of a friend. To be honest, it was intolerable. Those present didn't say a word; they saw nothing and heard almost nothing of what the priest, his back to the people, was doing at the altar.

But it is clear that the Mass according to the Missal of St Pius V is a very sacred thing. Moreover, it hasn't been abolished: it is still authorized for elderly priests in 'private' celebrations. And when I celebrate Mass using the Roman Canon, on occasion in Latin, what is it that makes my Mass different from that of the priests of Ecône, of the Salle Wagram or of Flavigny, priests of the same priesthood? Only one thing, but it is pregnant with meaning: they set the 'St Pius V' Mass up against that of Paul VI, which they refuse to celebrate; they use

33

their celebrations as a manifesto and a protest, a gesture of disobedience and even of defiance. My God! Is it really possible? Is this the way to 'eat the Lord's Supper' (cf. 1 Cor 11:20)?

EN ROUTE FOR A SCHISM?

Schism is a terribly grave word. Fr G. Cottier, a follower of the holy Cardinal Journet, wrote this summer: 'Mgr Lefebvre has taken the slippery path that leads to schism and perhaps to heresy.' A strange prognostication concerning a man who opposes the Pope and post-Vatican II Catholicism only in order to maintain an absolute fidelity to the 'perpetual' orthodoxy which the same Council is supposed to have betrayed! Yet there is a story about an Egyptian hermit who, in order to find even greater silence, went so far into the desert that he ended up by crossing it and coming out at the other side. But let's be serious.[15]

There are two classic definitions of schism: 'setting one altar up against another', and 'refusing to act as part of a whole'.

In our eucharistic celebrations we profess to be in communion 'with Paul our Pope' and with the local bishop. The Eucharist is the sacrament of unity; it signifies this unity and nourishes it. As the sacrament of the body of Christ, the Eucharist fulfils us as the Mystical Body ('Mystical' meaning mysterious, spiritual, ecclesial) by letting us share in the body of Christ made sacramentally present. So brotherly union is inseparable from union with Christ in the sacrament. The tangible criterion for brotherly union, for being in communion with the Church, is union with the local bishop who is himself in union with the other bishops and with the Bishop of Rome, centre of Catholic unity. Celebrating the Eucharist outside these rules for communion is tantamount to setting up one altar against another, to use the classic expression of the Fathers who had such a strong sense of the bond between Church and Eucharist. For example, here is what the bishop and martyr St Cyprian wrote in 251 while warning against the threat of schism:

> One must turn aside and flee from anyone who is separated from the Church: he is a pervert, a sinner who is damning himself. Does he believe that he remains united to Christ when he acts against Christ's priests, when he breaks away from his clergy and his people? He turns his weapons against the Church: he battles against divine ordinances. Adversary of the altar, rebelling against Christ's sacrifice, an enemy of the faith instead of remaining faithful to it, [...] he dares, in contempt of the bishops and priests of God, to set up another altar, to utter another prayer with illicit words. . . .[16]

When the sense of unity of a social body became associated with the sense of the bond between ecclesial unity and eucharistic celebration, that great mind, Cardinal Cajetan – the same Cajetan before whom, as Legate, Luther had been ordered to present himself in 1518 – formulated the notion of schism as the refusal to conduct oneself as part of a whole, *sese gerere ut partem, esse partem unius numero populi*.[17] A schismatic is someone who wants to think, pray, act – in a word, live – not in harmony with the whole Church, as a part in conformity with the whole and with the authority which presides over the whole, but according to his own rules and like an autonomous being. This can be conceived not only with regard to the whole that the Church actually is, but equally in relation to the whole constituted by the continuum of the individual's life in time, the continuum of his history.

Mgr Lefebvre actually wrote to the Abbé G. de Nantes on 19 March 1975: 'I would have you know that, if a bishop does break away from Rome, it won't be me' (*Un évêque parle*, p. 273). By that he understands faithful (according to his lights) Rome, 'Eternal Rome', not the Rome of Vatican II or the Rome of the Missal of Paul VI. But how can one claim to be right and claim to conduct oneself as part of a whole when one objects to the Eucharist that 700,000,000 Catholics, 400,000 priests and 2,550 bishops celebrate in union with the successor of Peter? Mgr Lefebvre said in a Luxembourg broadcast that the true Catholic Church is to be found at Ecône.[18] Can it be, then, that the others – the Pope – all of us – are actually schismatics? This is what Mgr Lefebvre maintains, for example in the course of several paragraphs of a text issued from Ecône on 2 August 1976 and published in the newspaper *Le Figaro* on 4 August. In another instance, during an interview with the Italian weekly *Europeo*, he said: 'It is not I who have activated a schism. It's the Church of Rome, the Church of the Council, which has separated itself from Christ.' And at Lille on 29 August 1976 he declared: 'We are not in a state of schism, for it is we who continue the Catholic Church. It is those who carry out the reforms who are in a state of schism.'

This is unthinkable. Surely it demands reconsideration.

In order to go more deeply into what is at issue, it seems best to go over the criticisms and rejections of the Council again, then to discuss the present crisis, and finally to state how we would wish to see the drama end.

2. An Evaluation of the Council

Of the reforms put in hand since the Council, reform of the Mass and the sacraments have been the most criticized and most rejected. We have already discussed this. Now we must devote our attention to other documents and conciliar positions which have equally been the subject of anathematization.

IS COLLEGIALITY AN ABOLITION OF AUTHORITY?

Mgr Lefebvre is not the only one to have drawn attention to the existence of a danger: that the personal exercise of authority will be diminished because of conferences, commissions, centralized organizations, national chaplaincies, etc. It really does not appear that collegiality and the setting-up of synods have overshadowed papal authority. Moreover, it is not apparent that senates of priests and, where they exist (there are very few in France), pastoral councils have eroded the authority of the bishop. But it *is* permissible to ask if obstinate public disobedience to local bishops and to the Pope doesn't threaten their authority.

What we understand by 'collegiality' really consists of two distinct things which are only bound together by the deep root of communion. The term 'collegial' has become trendy; it gets used in a broad and rather pragmatic sense: such-and-such a project, we say, has collegial guidance. As far as the Church is concerned, we sometimes say that collegiality has been lacking when a decision has been taken by someone in authority without consultation at grass-roots level. This is an incorrect usage of the word which we tolerate in order to speak about an authentic and traditional reality. The deep-seated tradition is, in fact, that the community co-operates in regulating its own life, not by usurping authority which is structured and differentiated, but by a whole system of advice, information, confident communicating from top to bottom and from bottom to top, between all the parties concerned.[19] The Church is a body: it has a head, but the whole of the body is alive.

A broad advisory system including consultation and concerted action is all the more desirable today when, on one hand, culture and information are so widespread and people are used to taking part in decisions and, on the other hand, problems are much more complex, involving many more far-reaching elements and, in the final analysis, because we don't have either models or precedents for many new problems. So communications are much easier these days. . . . The Church has everything to gain by developing her conciliar or collegial life in this broad meaning of the word.

The meaning of the word is much more restricted when the Council speaks of the College of Bishops – the word 'collegiality' is never used.[20] Here, the bishops form a body, structured too, with the successor of Peter at its head: this body has the responsibility of governing the Church, and therefore the power to do so. The power is fully exercised when the College undertakes a collegial act, i.e. a single act carried out together by the members of the College. This is what happened at the Council when the Bishop of Dakar and the Bishop of Chicago, together with all the others, made a decision affecting the whole Church – from Paris to Saigon. This is a deeply traditional reality, which Cyprian in 251 described in this unforgettable way: 'Episcopal dignity is one, and each bishop has it on his own account without dividing up the whole (*in solidum*).'[21]

Collegial acts, in the strict sense of the word, are rare. Councils are *incidents* in the life of the Church; they are not part of the usual run of things. However, as Mgr G. Philips put it, if the College is not in a state of acting collegially all the time, neither is it ever unemployed. This is where the broader idea of 'collegiality' comes in. As Paul VI said at the 1969 Synod, collegiality is communion, solidarity, co-responsibility. It is the translation, at the level of responsible pastors, of the communion and solidarity of the Churches. This is no longer a question of 'power', but it remains, and always will remain, a question of responsibility. No Christian can say 'Am I my brother's keeper?' (cf. Gen 4:9 – Cain); no Church can say 'I am rich, I lack nothing, I have no need of anyone else' (cf. Apoc 3:17). O great, holy, wonderful communion of the Church!

Men imbued with a conservative and paternalistic spirit ('Everything for the people, nothing by the people' said Donoso Cortès) have a kind of 'gut repulsion' for words like 'grass-roots', 'the people', 'democracy' – we haven't mentioned the last one: it works so badly when applied to the Church or in the context of the Church. This repulsion is a reaction governed by temperament and political persuasion. But the Church has its own order of things, and its essential nature – communion – goes back more than seventeen centuries before the time of the French Revolution and nineteen centuries before the Russian Revolution.[22] This has absolutely nothing to do with politics, but with Christian existence in the Church.

IS ECUMENISM A BETRAYAL OF TRUTH?

'We reject an ecumenism which betrays our Faith and our Holy Religion, which aims at uniting the Catholic Church to the errors of the world and to Protestant heresies.'[23]

I couldn't agree more; and neither could the Council – on condition that the words 'betrays' and 'aims' be replaced by 'would betray' and 'would aim', for the present phraseology suggests an accomplished fact. Now, we wouldn't deny that excesses do exist – we have even criticized them ourself – but this isn't the ecumenism of the Council. Excesses are fatal since ecumenism is a beginning, a movement – things which by their nature demand that one should go beyond them. We have to be on our guard, therefore, but we don't have to have closed minds. 'Faithfulness and openness', the motto of a movement animated by my friend Gérard Soulages, would be a pretty good motto for a healthy ecumenism.

If ecumenism were liberalism, 'confusionism', cheap mutual understanding and syncretism, how is one to explain that it tends to result in a revitalised awareness of what one actually believes in, at least at first? The answer to that, I suppose, will be that it's true for the others but not for the Catholics. Fr Bruckberger thinks that he can apply to French Protestants the résumé which President Kennedy produced of the Soviet position after his meeting with Kruschev: 'What we have is all our own, and no one's going to touch it. What you have is negotiable.'[24] To say this is to have a very poor knowledge of what is actually going on – a poor knowledge of our relationships and of the progression of ideas which, based on a fresh examination of bones of contention, is a slow but effective movement towards an agreement. It's quite possible that, since Catholics have a history which is far more loaded with dogmatism, they tend to reconsider things more. But I would ask you, Fr Bruckberger, what exactly is it that the Council and the Secretariat for Christian Unity have betrayed? I leave you the risky and even reprehensible task of answering this question. The whole thing boils down to serious and responsible ecumenism, the ecumenism of the Council. In my opinion it rests on these two bases: being open to the Spirit of God, and loving the truth.

Anyone who has become involved with the ecumenical movement, who has encountered serious and committed Christians there, cannot but believe that in our century, so problematical regarding the faith, God has raised up this movement like a huge tide that proclaims the attraction of a supreme heavenly body, the Holy Spirit, the 'Unknown beyond the Word' (H. U. von Balthasar), whose nature is to concentrate together people, energies and initiatives which do not even know of each others' existence. Of course this has to be carried out through the agency of men, and so it is all mixed up with dross and ambiguities. But something comes from God: it's the *fact* of the Holy Spirit, setting my open-mindedness in motion, who justifies my having a different attitude towards non-catholics (Cardinal Journet called them 'dissidents') from the attitude approved and practised in the past, even by authorities whom I revere.

In February 1939 I had a fairly extended conversation with Cardinal Baudrillat (the positions which he subsequently took up were already starting to become clear) in the course of which he tackled me vigorously: 'How is it that you Dominicans, who were once the Order of the Inquisition, have today become so friendly with Protestants and others?' I answered him from the depths of a belief which I still have: the two things are motivated by the same love of truth, but applied differently. The Dominicans thought at the time of the Inquisition that they held the whole truth in their hands, and anything which didn't agree with their fixed and defined orthodoxy had to be eliminated (they said 'ex-terminated' in the sense of 'banished'). As for me, I want to gather up every small fragment of truth, wherever it is to be found, with the same care that I would use in picking up a tiny piece of a consecrated host. This is the theological or doctrinal aspect of ecumenism. There are others, but this one dominates the rest and is above all the one which I am personally attached to. Its aim is to obtain simultaneously the purity and the fullness of truth. And who could deny that the Protestants might possess small fragments or elements of truth? Who would pretend that we have nothing to gain or rediscover? So, in praying ceaselessly – for an essential ingredient of ecumenism is a lot of prayer – we strive to realize the prayer that Jesus prayed between the Last Supper and the cross: 'That they all may be one as we are one.'

While maintaining a sense of proportion (or *positis ponendis*, as one might say in Latin), something analogous can be said about non-christian religions. Of course their position is different, and the Council was very cautious in its Declaration *Nostra aetate* of 28 October 1965. Moreover, that Declaration said – and this is a point on which Fr J. Daniélou was right to insist – that 'the Catholic Church . . . proclaims, and has ceaselessly made a point of proclaiming, that Christ is "the way, the truth and the life" (Jn 14:6) in which men must find the fullness of religious life and in which God reconciles all things to himself' (no. 2, para 2).

IS THE COUNCIL'S DECLARATION ON RELIGIOUS LIBERTY A CHARTER FOR INDIFFERENCE?

That document was a great battle. The minority, to which Mgr Lefebvre belonged, fought every inch of the way, developing serious arguments and proposing counter-projects. Error has no rights, the minority said, but here we are improperly putting it on the same footing as the truth. We are laying down the exact opposite of the Syllabus of Pius IX and other impressive documents.

These are not contemptible arguments. It is surprising, despite everything, that the text – at least, the final one to be proposed – should have aroused so much intense emotion. What does it actually say? It is false to claim that it suppresses the right of God to be listened to and obeyed, and the corresponding duty of men 'to seek out the truth, above all in those things concerning God and his Church, and, when they have discovered it, to embrace it and remain faithful to it' (no. 1, and cf. no. 3, para 1, and no. 14). It is false to claim that the Declaration doesn't speak of the *libertas Ecclesiae*, that liberty which the Church has from God to proclaim the Gospel and to live the life of the Church: cf. no. 10, no. 13 and no. 15, para 2. The affirmation of religious liberty is precisely this: 'That all men should be sheltered from all constraint, whether on the part of individuals or of social groupings or of any human power whatsoever, so that in religious matters no one should be compelled to act contrary to his conscience, nor prevented from acting – within reasonable limits – according to his conscience, in private or in public, alone or in association with others. The right to religious liberty has its foundation in the very dignity of the human person, such as has been

made known by the word of God and by reason itself'
(no. 2).

It cannot be denied that a text like this does *materially*
say something different from the Syllabus of 1864, and
even almost the opposite of propositions 15 and 77-9 of
that document. But among other things, the Syllabus
was trying to defend a temporal power which, taking
into account the new situation, the papacy renounced
in 1929. The historico-social context within which the
Church is called to live and to speak had changed, and
lessons had been learnt from circumstances. Catholics
had understood already in the nineteenth century that
the Church would gain more support for its freedom in
the affirmed belief of the faithful than in the favour of
princes. It is with feeling that I call to mind the
intellectual eminence and religious quality of Fr John
Courtney Murray, who demonstrated that from Leo
XIII, via Pius XI and above all Pius XII, to the John
XXIII of *Pacem in terris*, the popes have more and more
clearly and more and more resolutely pressed the claim
of the dignity of the human person against regimes and
other means of constraint, in such a way that the
Declaration on Religious Liberty follows in the wake of this
succession and represents the crowning point of a con-
tinuous movement.[25] The Declaration had every right
to say: 'In dealing with this religious liberty, the holy
Council sees the development of the doctrine of the
most recent Sovereign Pontiffs on the inviolable rights
of the human person and juridical order in society' (no.
1, at the end). Everything is centred on the value of the
person. 'Error has no rights.' Obviously, but these are
persons who do have rights; and those who are in error
guard the right, founded in their very nature, to remain
free from constraint in matters concerning their conscience.

One would be astonished that such a modest declaration should have given rise to so much discussion if one didn't know how much the weight of centuries of Christianity still bore down on some excellent minds. Not everybody admitted the movement of history or the positions taken up by J. Maritain in *Humanisme intégral* (*True Humanism*) (1935). Fully Catholic Maritain (who even wanted a recognition of the 'indirect power' of the Church over the City) also held that the whole of human life, social and personal, must be placed in submission to God and orientated towards his Kingdom. The real question is to know what kind of action or influence the Church should exercise on society as such. The Church has known a system of acting by power and ordinance; in those days she was able to penalize failure to obey her regulations by laws and police measures. This gave rise to the Inquisition and, the final episode in France under Charles X, the blasphemy law and the case pleaded by Odilon Barrot. The Church will never give up proclaiming that Jesus is Lord and doing everything possible to orientate the temporal world towards God and according to the laws of God. But in an already pluralistic world which the general mix of men, information and ideas makes fatally pluralistic, above all in a world where the properly Christian value of the person is affirmed as inviolable, the Church wants to exercise an influence on persons, through persons, through the channel of their beliefs and the force of truth itself. 'Influence' signifies a real action without 'power'. Now is the time for bearing witness and for evangelic signs born of a total love.

It's some time now since the Church went over to this form of action, but it has not happened everywhere at the same time. There are certain people who have preserved a nostalgia for Christianization by power –

what Etienne Gilson described as the nostalgia for a new baptism by Clovis. By the *Declaration on Religious Liberty*, by the Pastoral Constitution *Gaudium et spes, On the Church in the Modern World*, – a significant title, this! – the Church of Vatican II has openly placed herself in the pluralist world of today; and, without disowning anything great that there may have been, has cut the ropes which were mooring her to the banks of the Middle Ages. You cannot stay *stuck* at a particular moment in history.

Mgr Lefebvre speaks of 'the Reign of Our Lord Jesus Christ over persons, over families and over civil societies'. One would have thought it was Pius X or Pius XI who was speaking. But the question is one of knowing by what means and in what form this reign should be promoted and obtained. The text we have just quoted, which comes from the letter of 17 July 1976 to Paul VI, continues: 'He [Your Holiness] will restore their proper perspective to the falsified ideas which have become the idols of modern man: liberty, equality, fraternity, democracy'. We suspect that the reign of Jesus Christ will have to be established on the invalidation or the repeal of democracy (and why not of the Edict of Nantes?). But the Lille speech of 29 August makes the thing much clearer and more positive. The actual model is Argentina.

. . . Take the example of the Argentine Republic. What kind of a state was it in only two or three months ago? Complete anarchy . . . brigands killing to left and right, industries utterly ruined, factory-owners locked up or taken as hostages. [. . .]

But now there is an orderly government which has principles, which has authority, which is starting to tidy things up, which is stopping brigands from killing other people; and the economy is actually starting to revive, and the workers have actually got work to do, and they can actually go home knowing that they are not going to be brained on the way by someone who wants to make them go on strike when they don't want to go on strike. (*Le Monde*, 31 August 1976)

But in Argentina an authority with blood on its hands is physically suppressing those who oppose it. Who can think that is right and proper?

TRUE AND FALSE IDEAS ABOUT TRADITION

Here we come to a decisive point. Mgr Lefebvre never stops invoking tradition. He said to the Pope, 'Allow us simply to use the experience of tradition'. If the only meaning of that was 'Allow us to train priests according to the tried and tested rules of bygone days, but accepting the Council and the reforms which it got under way', there would be no problem, or at any rate no problem of principle. Perhaps it could even be acknowledged that such a priestly formation complies very well with the conciliar Decree *Optatam totius Ecclesiae renovationem* of 28 October 1965, *On the Formation of Priests*. But this is not what Mgr Lefebvre is asking for. For him, tradition is what he calls 'Eternal Rome', 'the Mass as it has always been' – in other words, Rome up to and excluding Paul VI, up to and excluding the Missal of 1969.

However, he has a good passage on tradition in his text of 2 August 1976, which expressed the most hardened rejection of the Council and the Pope (*Le Figaro*, 4 August): 'The Catholic Church is a Mystic Reality which exists not only in space, on the surface of the earth, but also in time and in eternity. In order for the Pope to represent the Church and be the image of Her, he must not only be united to Her in space but also in time, *the Church being essentially a living tradition.*' Perhaps a man who has published three books on tradition[26] might be allowed to italicize these last words and put these questions:

Did life, of which the Holy Spirit is the supreme author, cease in the Church in 1962? Is life lacking in the Catholic communion ratified by the 2,500 bishops who surround the successor of Peter? *Securus iudicat orbis terrarum* said St Augustine in a well-known text: the whole universe is a good criterion.

By continually referring back to the Mass of St Pius V (1570), to the catechism of the Council of Trent (1566) and the catechism of St Pius X (1912), isn't Mgr Lefebvre battoning up tradition in the formulae of the past, certainly sacred and valuable formulae but nevertheless formulae which, *on the plane of formulation*, cannot forbid the search for a better adaptation to the needs of today? It goes without saying that such an adaptation, an *aggiornamento*, mustn't betray the faith. It is possible that this might be the case with some disordered initiative or other – and we will come back to this point – but no serious argument could maintain that such disorder existed in the case of the Council itself, nor in the case of the Missal of Paul VI.

The Church is tradition, the handing-down of what has been given once and for all: revelation, sacraments and ministry. It's therefore easy to understand that a sincere and faithful body of Catholics is attached to one form or another of this tradition. Those who are in sympathy with categorical, trenchant declarations will give pride of place to the forms which reflect this need. But the great river of tradition is wider than a straight canal with cemented parapets. The tradition of the

Fathers is richer than the tradition whose content was fixed in the face of the Reformation by the 'Holy Council of Trent' (when I was a boy, my parish priest always used to use this expression). The Holy Spirit did not abandon the Church from 1962 onwards, or from 1965! Let us be fully catholic Catholics together with, yes, the eternal Church – that of Vatican II like that of Trent or Nicea, the Church of Paul VI like that of Pius V like that of the Pope St Marcel (who died in 309)!

3. The present Crisis

The crisis is a real one – I know that. A large amount of correspondence received as the result of an article about Ecône (in *La Croix*, 20 August 1976) made me realize even more that there is quite a deep-seated malaise in large areas of the lay faithful. I am certainly not the only one for whom the Ecône-Lefebvre affair will at least have had the benefit of provoking a sharper and more enlightened self-examination on various aspects of the crisis, even though I had already thought deeply about it.

IS THE COUNCIL RESPONSIBLE FOR THE CRISIS?

The answer to this question, put in such general terms, must be a resolute No. If the Council, its Constitution *Dei Verbum* on Divine Revelation, its Decrees on the formation, life and ministry of priests, on the lay apostolate – in fact the whole of its guidances – were really followed, we wouldn't have this particular crisis on our hands. Others dispute this and propose the Church in Poland as an example: a Church which would be very annoyed if she thought that she was suspected of not implementing the Council. But she doesn't have the opportunity to abuse facilities and freedom like we do. Maybe we were too optimistic in packing our bags to return home after the Council. Perhaps certain documents were already out of date and irrelevant to the actual situation. But shouldn't parents nevertheless be restrained in their reproaches – those parents who have given their children a Christian, open, social and generous upbringing, only to see them rejecting religious marriage, omitting to baptize their babies, and walking along a path which Bernard Besret would describe as 'deviance'?

'You judge a tree by its fruits' . . . but aren't we mistaking the identity of this tree? Are these the fruits *of the Council*? On the contrary, shouldn't we be crediting the Council with some marvellous results? Think about all those beautiful celebrations, the spreading of the word of God, the vitality of local Churches, the revived awareness of social responsibilities. . . .

However, we don't deny that the Council has played a part in what has grown into the crisis. One could classify this under four main aspects:

1. Discussion has taken place. That's true of all Councils, but this time the discussions have been bruited abroad, blown up, amplified. The reasonably fictitious notion of a monolithic, self-assured Church with an answer to everything has been lost.

2. The Church has opened her doors and windows and a new wind has blown in. This is very significant, but we won't expand on it here as we shall be coming back to it a bit further on.

3. By the frankness and openness of its debates, the Council has put an end to what may be described as the inflexibility of the system. We take 'system' to mean a coherent set of codified teachings, casuistically-specified rules of procedure, a detailed and very hierarchic organization, means of control and surveillance, rubrics regulating worship – all this the legacy of scholasticism, the Counter-reformation and the Catholic

51

Restoration of the nineteenth century, subjected to an effective Roman discipline. It will be recalled that Pius XII is supposed to have said: 'I will be the last Pope to keep all this going.' Indeed, John XXIII, a priest of classic piety, gave a completely different image to the papacy. The great conciliar coming together, the meetings, the availability of information on many questions, the necessary pursuit of an *aggiornamento* – all this brought an end to what we have called the inflexibility of the system. On the other hand, there are those who recall that system with nostalgia. . . .

4. It's dishonest to take advantage of the fact that the Council wanted to be, and declared itself to be, 'pastoral' in order to accuse it of not having been doctrinal. From its very beginnings, and at the Council itself, this false imputation was rebutted. But there is a grain of truth in Mgr Graber's remark[27] that, due to its 'pastoral' character and its broad outlook which wasn't riddled with precise Canons of the *Anathema sit* variety, the Council was able to promote movements which went beyond the Council itself. It is quite right to talk about 'the dynamism of the Council', but sometimes this is too easily complained about.

THE CRISIS AS THE IMPACT IN THE CHURCH OF AN INCREDIBLE CHANGE IN CIVILIZATION AND OF CRITICAL QUESTIONS NEGLECTED FOR TOO LONG

To my way of thinking, this is the principal point. To put it briefly, ferments in culture and social life have developed in the modern world – a world which was for too long shut out of a Church on the defensive – and came pouring in in torrents through the open doors:

and all this at a time when the world was undergoing an unbelievable mutation which nobody at the moment is able to master. A little further on we will be providing the necessary documentary justification, but in the meantime we will examine the elements of this long and unwieldy statement in order to make them comprehensible.

Whatever anyone may say, a modern world exists. Whether one counts it as beginning in the sixteenth century (the Renaissance and the Reformation, which will be considered separately), or round about 1680 (as Paul Hazard does in his always illuminating books), or in the eighteenth century with the 'Age of Enlightenment', doesn't matter much. In any case the movement continued logically between all these periods. In 1784 Kant defined the Age of Enlightenment as 'the emergence of Man from his infancy, an emergence for which he himself is responsible. "Infancy" means his incapability of making use of his understanding in the direction of others.' On the basis of a whole series of research, questionings and significant works, the explanation of these things has been sought – and often found – not above, in heaven, but below, in the things themselves and in Man. Yes, Man has become the centre and the reference-point for everything. With the French Revolution, and after it, the movement, which at first affected only the cultivated classes, had its social expression. Daniel-Rops gave the title *L'Eglise des révolutions* [The Church of upheavals] to his book devoted to this period (it was written after *L'ère des grands craquements* [The era of large splittings]). In the event, this was the era of 1830, 1848, the Communist manifesto of Marx, the '71 Commune, the workers' movement – the response to an inhuman industrialization.

It's clear that the Church couldn't accept Man as the reference-point for Man, nor the rationalist rejection of any transcendental and supernatural intervention. She therefore engaged in a tough 'combat for God' (another of Daniel-Rops' titles). Involved in formidable attacks, sometimes even to the point where her very existence was threatened, the Church locked herself up as if in a besieged castle, all doors barred and drawbridges raised, while all the time carrying out a powerful restoration of her internal forces and an exceptional missionary expansion. She closed herself not only to antitheistic anthropocentrism but also to real problems, to genuine acquisitions in the realm of thought. What did Pius IX, who enjoyed the longest pontificate in history, have to say about all the questions which characterized the period – the workers' movement, Communism, colonialism, historical and biblical criticism, etc? Certainly Leo XIII had something to say, but his beginnings, so real in certain areas, were not nearly as great as people have sometimes claimed. The modernism which was coming to light at the end of his pontificate was certainly worthy of reproof, but instead he posed valid questions which have not been resolved; and to a certain extent he has been linked with various movements, such as the philosophy of Maurice Blondel or the biblical research of Fr Lagrange, which had nothing to do with him except insofar as they were contemporary with him. A besieged citadel, closed and on the defensive: wasn't the Church running the risk of being like the American Indians – a protected reservation, but a separated one? The risk was not an obvious one because of the Church's observable great internal vitality and because, by her schools and her works, by her laity (Albert de Mun's ACJF [French Youth Catholic Action movement], the 'action of Catholics'

54

under Pius X, Action Catholique of the time of Pius XI), she had a presence in society. But the Church remained apart, regulated by the system that we have already mentioned.

The flood-gates were opened and the water came rushing in. The ice melted, and this was the onset of a rapid thaw. Doors and windows were opened and the wind swept in. These are only mental pictures, and doubtless too simplistic and too overdone. We could show – and we have a dossier on the subject – that many of the movements with which to a greater or lesser extent we are preoccupied today were starting in the 1950s: drop in the number of vocations, small spontaneous groups, liturgical reforms, philosophical questionings, so-called 'new theology', ecumenism, growing diffusion of existential attitudes giving pride of place to autonomy and the spontaneity of the individual, etc, etc. But all that, for what it's worth, was contained within a disciplined Church. There was too much that was true and too much that was necessary, there were too many values necessitated by general development, for the new waves not to find their way through. When, after the red light and then the amber, the green light was given by John XXIII's Council, the waves in the Church grew bigger. The Rhine didn't have to flow into the Tiber, as Ralph M. Wiltgen put it. All that was necessary was, that instead of being a ghetto, the People of God, making their way along the roads of men, should take up a full dialogue with the world once again.

Which world, then? The world is in a complete state of flux. The Church, sitting in Council, felt this; the Introduction to the Pastoral Constitution *Gaudium et spes, On the Church in the Modern World*, briefly describes this state of change, but that was in 1965. Since then we have witnessed a mad, galloping urbanization, and in France we watched the rebellion of the young with the student riots of May 1968. As J.-L. Barrault says, the storm smote Paris in this month, but it came from afar and has continued to prowl around the earth. Separated by only a few months, this world event took place in Tokyo, Los Angeles, Santiago . . . as well as in Paris; it reached Rome and even Warsaw. The movement is critical of everything which smells of institution, of 'the establishment', of anything which tries to impose itself on men without those men having themselves decided upon it. It's something else, too: a need to find oneself again, a priority given to the future rather than to the past, a frenetic joy without need of transcendence, a sexual liberation; it's the presence of world-shaking events in one's consciousness; it's disgust with and criticism of the structures of domination. And what does the impact of the human sciences have to say on religious reflection? There are real questions here which cannot be resolved with a shrug of the shoulders. We do not seek to give a complete and ordered analysis; but it's this world that we have to deal with. Often at the end of conferences, in questions from the floor, this kind of criticism is heard: 'It seems that the seminarians are such-and-such, or are doing such-and-such a thing.' I ask in reply: 'Monsieur, Madame, what are *your* children doing?' 'Oh! They're always challenging things, our children are . . .'. Alas, we don't have any other children: your son could be a seminarian. . . .

Often enough, the end-product is characterized by a break with the past, which runs the risk of being a break with tradition. We can't accept that. A historian like Pierre Chaunu never stops telling us that Man can only broach his future if he admits his past. This is very true, expressed in historical terms. In theological terms, it's the tradition which must be examined. Tradition isn't the past, it isn't old habits kept up by *esprit de corps*. Tradition is actuality, simultaneously handing on, receiving and creating. Tradition is the presence of a principle at every moment of its development. We don't accept the break. The Church never stops innovating, by the grace of the Holy Spirit, but she always takes from the roots and makes use of the sap which comes from them. In the beautiful words of Gertrud von Le Fort: 'Man must always have earth under his feet, otherwise his heart dries up.'[28]

REGRETTABLE MALPRACTICES – INADMISSIBLE ANARCHY

I still maintain that the principal cause of the present crisis lies in the impact which the questions, struggles and changes that affect world society have had on the People of God. Some of my friends – for example Gérard Soulages or André Piettre – have told me that in their opinion I am minimizing the abuses and omissions of Catholic regulations regarding celebration, catechesis, preaching and pastoral practice. My reaction to these things comes from not wanting to generalize; I would by no means deny that malpractices exist but, having knowledge as I do of so many loyal efforts and of so many irreproachable priests, I didn't want to use all-embracing formulations of the sort typified by '*Priests* don't believe in . . . any longer', or '*Nobody* preaches about sin or grace any more', or even '*They* are destroying the faith of our children'. Because of their vagueness and their generalization, accusations such as these appeared to me, and still do appear to me, to be grossly unfair.[29] Furthermore, it seemed to me that they fought shy of recognizing the decisive influence, in the present crisis, of the world crisis in civilization and society, as well as avoiding genuine questions and objective difficulties which lie heavily on the faith of believers.

The insistence of my friends, the letters received as a result of my *La Croix* article, and the letters published in that paper, have all led me to a greater awareness of the uneasiness evoked in the minds of many Catholics by certain debatable fantasies and by the standard of celebrations, sermons and catechesis. This summer's drama, between Mgr Lefebvre on one side and the Pope and bishops on the other, could have the benefit of making people take this uneasiness, felt by many of the faithful, more seriously. In a way, Mgr Lefebvre has given them a voice, even if his voice does not really represent what they are actually thinking. Not everything is of the same seriousness in their grievances, and it appears possible to arrange them in three main categories:

1. For some people, it's an allergy to any kind of change. When Pius XII reformed the celebration of holy days and restored the Paschal Vigil, they were already saying 'Our religion is being changed!' The natural and, in itself, respectable need to look for a sense of security in religion is here being transformed into a yearning for hanging on to what you're accustomed to; it makes you feel cosy. Or equally, it can be a question of things which are praiseworthy in themselves but which offend a poorly-enlightened emotional sensitivity: such a person will complain, for instance, that people are singing the praises of 'that heretic' Martin Luther King, or that a woman with uncovered head is reading from the lectern, or that young people are accompanying the Mass with jazz percussion. . . .

2. Among the things which people give me as examples, and against which they fulminate, some are merely regrettable and are not really serious in themselves. Thus, for instance, the priest who, before celebrating Mass, goes into the body of the church to explain what is going to happen, dressed in polo-neck sweater or T-shirt. I'm not saying that this is all right, but it's not something to get so tremendously worked-up about. In fact, I attach some importance to the priest, if about to celebrate Mass, even in a private house, putting on a vestment which signifies that here we no longer have Mr X but a minister of Christ and the Church. The minimum for a sign of this function is the stole.

Another example: the priest, or even the bishop, who says 'The Church today isn't juridical any more but mystical' – and just leaves it at that. This is too simple an affirmation, and one that needs explaining in any circumstances and which could, if misinterpreted, give rise to false ideas.

3. There remain malpractices which are objectively regrettable and reprehensible. There are three principal fields: (a) the liturgy; (b) theology or catechesis; (c) a certain trend towards politics.

(a) People call attention to a certain liturgical anarchy. My *confrère* Fr Auvray analyzes five publications in which can be found a total of 103 Eucharistic Prayers, some of which do not, he says, fully express the faith of the Church.[30] Another *confrère*, Fr Bruckberger, takes up the same reproach in the 29 July 1976 issue of *L'Aurore*. In his article of 19 August 1976 this figure swells to 300 Canons. This is going too far. It's true that in the early Church the Eucharistic Prayer didn't exist in a fixed written state – St Justin in about A.D. 50

59

says that the president of the assembly (in Greek the *proestos*) 'offers up prayers and thanksgivings as well as he is able'[31] – but Fr Louis Bouyer has shown that liturgical creativity in ancient times followed fairly precise models.[32] By any standards, a Eucharistic Prayer should express the faith of the Church and include, according to the best-established tradition, a thanksgiving for the benefits of creation and the redemption, an epiclesis (invocation of the Holy Spirit), the institution narrative, and an anamnesis (recalling redemptive acts, from the Passion to the glorification of Christ). If we're talking about a parish celebration, the faithful have the right to find in it what they expect to find, without being taken aback, and still less shocked by an irregular innovation.

Several correspondents are especially concerned with the ACO [Workers' Catholic Action] celebrations at the Porte de Versailles or, more recently, the celebrations of the JOC [Young Catholic Workers] apprentices. I don't want to defend something which could turn out to be indefensible. I didn't attend any of these celebrations, but neither am I part of the working class. Faced with a particular position, or a specific declaration, I have often stopped myself from passing judgement, telling myself that if I was in this situation I would probably do or say the same. . . .

(b) The plea addressed to the Holy Father on 8 August 1976 by several authors (Michel Ciry, Michel Droit, Gustave Thibon, etc) said: 'The faithful are no longer able to recognize their religion in certain liturgies and in certain pastoral practices. Even less are they able to recognize it in the catechism which their children are now being taught, in the contempt for basic morals, in the heresies professed by prominent theologians, in the politicization of the Gospel.' Which heresies? Which theologians? To speak, not about catechesis in which I do not have sufficient competence,[33] but about theology which I am in close touch with, I would say three things:

(1) There have been excesses, there have been publications open to criticism and some of these have been reprimanded; but honestly the number of such things has been tiny.

(2) These things have been criticized, both by other theologians and by the competent bishops. Personally, I attach a great deal of importance to criticism of theologians by their colleagues: I do it myself and, equally, I myself am subject to it!

(3) There exist real and difficult questions which theologians must have the courage to tackle – such as those on Christ's knowledge and awareness, on the way of talking about the resurrection, or on problems of sexuality – and for which it really isn't enough simply to repeat the old viewpoints. Theologians are themselves responsible for what they propose, and criticizing their thought is not only legitimate but useful. Such criticism should not be hasty, biased or excessive, for this runs the risk not only of destroying research which may be necessary but also of not understanding the real aims of such research. It also happens sometimes that imperfect thought may contain things of great richness which it would be very damaging to smother – for example in the case of Teilhard de Chardin.

(c) As regards politicization, this is a reality. In my view it is full of risks, but it can't really be discussed without looking at it more closely.

One complaint which one often hears is that 'priests' – once again a generalization – no longer preach on the mysteries of the faith but talk about Vietnam, Chile, strikes, trade unions, etc. Erstwhile Action Catholique movements, or at any rate Church movements, are supposed to have become branches of the Socialist or Communist Parties. In fact one does see catechetical teams actually subscribing to, for example, 'the socialist option', to say nothing of the Vie Nouvelle [New Life] which isn't (or isn't any longer) a Church movement, or of the MRJC [Young Catholics' Rural Movement], certain of whose members adopt Marxism as a tool for social analysis. It seems to me indisputable that a certain number of Catholics have adopted elements from Marxism, either as a method of social analysis or historical evaluation, or as a yardstick of revolutionary practice. An eminent parish priest actually said to me that it was intellectuals, people who write and speak, who do this and not people at grass-roots level. But aren't those who write and speak also leaders?

Independently of all this, the postconciliar Church is accused of having let herself be converted to the world. The voice of Jacques Maritain (*Le paysan de la Garonne* [*The Peasant of the Garonne*], 1966) is now being relayed, but at a higher pitch, by the voice of Maurice Clavel. The latter never wearies of quoting, as an example of the thought of a conciliar Father, a passage from Paul VI's speech at the closure of the fourth period of the Council (7 December 1965), completely removing it from its context and from the qualifications which make the meaning clear. The passage is this: 'The religion of God made Man has met up with the religion (for there is such a one) of Man who makes himself God. What happened? A sudden shock, a struggle, an anathema?

That could have happened, but it did not. [...] We also, more than anyone, possess the cult of Man. ...' Taking this as a basis, Fr G. de Nantes, formed in the thought of Maurras [the founder of Action Catholique] is trying to institute proceedings for heresy against Pope Paul VI. As far as what there is of Paul VI in it is concerned, the context is that of the *Humanisme intégral* of the Maritain of 1935. However, we do not deny that for Catholics today there exists the danger of reducing transcendent dimensions to the terrestrial, to the level of Man in his historical existence. Sometimes this even reaches as far as the liturgy: a little while ago, I heard of a *Gloria in excelsis* which was transformed into a hymn of praise – praise for that marvel that we men are!

If there is deviance, this has not arisen as a result of betrayal, but from a desire to live the requirement of the Gospel – love and service of men, as in Matthew 25:31–46: 'I was hungry ..., I was naked. ...' With others, Christians have discovered the effective and practical exigencies of what André Neher, commenting on Amos, calls the Justice of the Covenant. A laity invited to bring the mission of the Church into the temporal world is bound to ask questions and bound to want to speak the language of its undertakings. So – one part of the People of God, priests and faithful, cannot conceive of its Christianity without a trade-union-type of militancy and a political militancy, while another part of the same People of God takes exception to this orientation and accuses the others of 'being political'.

Experience shows that people articulate this griev-ance against the others when those others have chosen an opposing or different option. The universal watch-word these days is that everybody is acting politically: those who claim not to be doing this are actually doing it, at least in the sense that they are in favour of the status quo.[35] It is sometimes said that all men are equal but some are more equal than others! Could one say that everybody is dabbling in a political way but some are doing it more than others? At any rate, the facts are there: just as the crisis in the Church is principally due to the impact in the Church of the overall crisis of civilization and society, so the opposition between Left and Right is having its repercussions in the Church. Taking it to an extreme, there would be two Churches; for two conceptions of the faith and the kind of worship that one should render to God would exist – a dogmatic faith, an orthodox faith based on history, a faith of orthopraxis, with a ceremonial, sacerdotal form of worship; and a form of worship related to earthly justice, in the spirit of the prophets.[36]

Of course we can't accept such a division. The fact that it would equally affect Protestant communions, that it would establish in the ecumenical movement a differentiation between a theological ecumenism and a secular ecumenism often described as 'post-ecumenism', cannot detract anything at all from the truth of the transcendence of Jesus Christ, of his Gospel and of his Body which is the Church. Hence the necessity for a statute of pluralism and the falsity of insisting on a 'partisan' Church:[37] except that she must indeed defend and promote the cause of Man and that, in the choice of analyses or possible options, not all of these are of the same value with regard to the Gospel. In taking the part of the human person, which nowadays is often carried out in a very burdensome manner, a really committed Church will inevitably come up against the opposition of those who maintain structures of exploitation and oppression, and even against the opposition of her sons who in point of fact are in agreement with

these tendencies. The antagonisms of world society are thus to be found in the Church – a sign that she is no longer a separated ghetto. But how can her unity be preserved? At least two conditions are essential:
(i) that the Church must be the Church – nothing else, but truly and fully. This must be the work of everyone, but it is particularly on the shoulders of the clergy.
(ii) That in the People of God the conditions of political pluralism must genuinely be honoured. Some people object on this point.[38]

Here we have only been able to give a brief run-down on a set of very difficult and complex problems. We don't claim to have exhausted the topic, but merely to have 'placed', without undue simplisticism, the question of politicization which plays its part in the current crisis. A lady wrote this to me: 'The Church is having to learn the price of political options, or even of liturgical and social options, which come from authentic change according to the Gospel.' That's not a bad summing-up!

4. Towards a Solution

It would appear that no one is able to control the present situation, neither the bishops nor the Holy Father – both of whom, however, are leading the fight for fidelity and unity in the face of storms from East and West. Jesus alone can calm the storm; neither Peter nor the apostles could do so (cf. Matt 8:23–7 and parallel passages). In the present circumstances, what does this appeal for help to Jesus Christ mean for us? First of all, it seems to me, the Church must be the Church, and she should be so via a renewed attention to the Word of God.

THE CHURCH MUST BE THE CHURCH!

First and foremost, the Church is the faith: a faith which is lived, professed, liturgically celebrated (the sacraments) and preached. This faith is inseparable from a fundamental attitude of openness to God – 'credo *in* Deum', we believe *in the direction of God* – and *credo*: to determine the content of faith. This faith requires the real existence of two qualities, purity and fullness, between which a tension can exist. Purity is tested by a return to normative origins; fullness demands a lucid fidelity to the authentic development undergone by the faith in the life of the Church through space and time. It's here that tradition is located; it's here that the Fathers have pride of place. Even though it didn't produce any dogmas in the strict sense of the word, Vatican II, helped by the Holy Spirit, expressed the faithfulness of the Church at that moment in its history.

What is asked for, then, is a greater rigour in the conformity of catechesis, preaching and teaching, with reference to the norms of the faith of the Church. This cannot be the task of the authorities alone. Today, when the principle of personal belief is better recognized, all must be – and must feel themselves to be – personally responsible for their brothers. Additionally, the desire for purity must welcome the search for fullness, this search including new avenues for exploration, an openness to what new-found cultures can give, and an openness to the possibilities of ecumenical dialogue.

The Church is the love that the Spirit of God puts into our hearts – a love which seeks reconciliation and unity; an active love, inventive in initiatives of service; a deep love which in the compassion of God takes upon itself the pains of men by prayer and intercession. The Church is invited, in order to *be* the Church, unceasingly to return to the heart, to this interiorization which, far from turning men away, makes them become part of the Church in a way quite different from that of a facile and superficial secularization.

And the Church is mission – which is not the same as propaganda or proselytizing. It's a question of making available to all men, in their personal and social life, the benefits of the Gospel and of the grace of which the Church is, as it were, the sacrament. By comparison with the immensity of this missionary task and the unselfishnesses to be found in its service, our disputes are mean and shabby, outdated and sterile!

Yes, let the Church be the Church: nothing else, nothing more, but nothing less. 'I am not ashamed of the Gospel' said St Paul (Romans 1:16); 'I glory in the cross of our Lord Jesus Christ' (Galatians 6:14). What greater treasure could we bring to the world? But it's not an easy task. This treasure is too great for our strength, and we carry it – as St Paul again says – in earthen vessels: this symbolizes precariousness, but also the employment of all the different forms that this earth offers us and that history calls for in putting them at our disposal. The Church is the Church of God among men and on the path that men tread: not divinization, not secularization, but incarnation! It is the Church of the Word-made-flesh.

PRIMACY AND FERTILITY OF THE WORD OF GOD

The Church of the Word! The Council produced two dogmatic constitutions, *Lumen gentium*, *On the Church*, and *Dei verbum*, *On Divine Revelation*, scripture and tradition. Now, though the first has been read and commented upon, the second is insufficiently well known and followed. Naturally we can praise the vitality of biblical science. The way in which scripture is taught is incomparably superior to what it was, even up to the last war. We have plenty of excellent translations. The renewed liturgy offers a great wealth of readings; and homilies, frequently, explain them well. Many of the faithful are familiar with the sacred scriptures. In short, the overall picture is clearly a positive one, and yet there are still things which are lacking.

Is the Word of God, taken overall throughout its historical forward movement, the essential inspiration of theology as *Dei verbum* (no. 24) said it should be? Is it the nourishment and the guiding rule of all the Church's teaching and preaching (no. 21)? Granted that the Holy Father's allocutions at the Wednesday general audience are spiritually profound and nourished by holy scripture; but wouldn't many other official pronouncements gain much in force, and doubtless in the numbers of those who pay attention to them, if they followed more closely the divine teaching, taken throughout its forward historical movement, of which the scriptures are the witness?

Péguy once said that there isn't an abstract word in the Bible. What has been acquired over the centuries – the Fathers, the councils, the great works of scholarship – can certainly not be reduced by a kind of economy-drive; but, by following scripture, anything redolent of ideology can be avoided. Scripture is concrete. Scripture often teaches by means of stories and parables. . . .

From the first days of his pontificate, and several times later on, John XXIII urged the Church's ministers to be ministers of the Divine Book (his own phraseology):

Isn't the primordial task of the Catholic priesthood to communicate the great doctrine of the two Testaments and to make it penetrate into souls and into life? . . . Even though all the preoccupations of pastoral ministry are in our heart and our mind, we nevertheless feel that it is especially incumbent on us to evoke always and everywhere an enthusiasm for all the revelations of the Divine Book, whose function is to enlighten the path of life, from infancy to the most advanced age.[39]

Indeed, we can, we should *all* be found, receptive and overwhelmed, in the school of God's Word. All the declarations that we have quoted, and the humble discussions in this book, are immeasurably surpassed by the Word of God. Whether we are seminarians at Ecône or spectators at the Lille Mass, whether we are pilgrims in Rome or the faithful at a parish celebration, we are all and in the same way subject to the Word of God and judged by it. At least this Word, elucidated in Catholic tradition, is not open to discussion. It is a path to unity. What are we doing about it?

TEACHING AND EXPLAINING

Several people have written to me, saying that neither the Council nor the liturgical, catechetical or pastoral reforms which followed it were adequately explained. It's necessary to add something to this. I myself have known of several cases where the faithful complained that nobody told them about anything, when in fact a number of sermons and instruction-sessions had been given. But I also know of cases where the liturgical reforms were announced brutally, as a *fait accompli*, in force from that point in time onwards, to which it was necessary to submit – all without people's minds being prepared or any explanation being given.

The Council is still little known. It's not the only thing to have been 'disinherited'. In spite of so many efforts and so much service rendered by publishing houses and the Press, ignorance about religion is still widespread and deep-seated. And who knows of everything that the Pope says – I mean what he really says, without distortion? An enormous effort still needs to be made in order to inform, enlighten and instruct.

One of the things which is most lacking is a knowledge of history. Given a smattering of historical culture, the incomprehensible quarrel over the Mass would not have come about. History is a great school of intelligence and wisdom. Historical knowledge enables one to avoid making absolutes of what is relative, enables one to put things in their proper place, to sort out old tussles and ill-founded bones of contention. The crisis that we are presently suffering can be cleared up by history. It's obviously impossible to expect everybody to have the knowledge of a specialist but one may wish that in the necessary teaching effort, a place be made for the historical dimension of the issues.

AVOIDING A SECTARIAN SPIRIT

In France today, this spirit is raging in the form of a firmly-established Manichaeism. Manichaeism, as we know, describes the heresy which admits of two principles, one good and one bad, at the origin of things. In the same way, there exist the 'goodies' on one side – and to them everything is marvellous – and on the other side the 'baddies' – for whom everything is terrible. People are also still a bit animistic. They like to explain what causes them pain, or simply displeases them, by means of an evil occult principle: for Hitler it was the Jews and a Judaeo-Masonic plot. Those opposed to the Council are very ready to believe in some conspiracy or other: a 'Trojan horse', an organized pressure-group, Freemasonry. . . . Mgr Graber's pamphlet, already mention in footnote 2, gives them plenty of ammunition with which to do so.

Have I blackened those I have criticized? Any discussion runs the risk of not doing justice to the opposing party, to its rationale and to the exact meaning of its statements. If I am guilty of that, I apologize and am ready to correct myself. For me, Mgr Lefebvre and his disciples are brothers. We are in disagreement, and I believe that they are making a mistake; but I respect their intentions and their desire for fidelity. Nevertheless, I fear that they have reached a point where this desire is allied to a stubborn refusal to give way and an obstinate self-righteousness in the face of all the facts. If they will listen to me, if I am not in their eyes irretrievably situated in the opposing camp (of baddies) – I would implore them to cast emotion aside. It so often happens in squabbles between family or friends that the squabble feeds on itself as it goes on. The original cause is still there, but it has become hardened by pigheadedness and has passed the point of no return.

A remedy *must* therefore be found. Couldn't a kind of moratorium be agreed upon? Cardinal Suenens asked the Abbé J. Kamp, 'a devoted and generous priest whose sincerity is indisputable', if he would not 're-examine himself before the Lord'. A number of his confrères helped him in this by means of a dialogue which is a model of goodwill and intelligence (cf. footnote 34 above). Couldn't something similar be possible? It has often been said that an internal ecumenism is necessary in today's Church. From an objective point of view, this should be less difficult than the other kind of ecumenism since we have many more points of reference in common. Indeed, we have (nearly) everything in common! But it would be necessary to unclench our muscles and, with the help of God, arm ourselves with a very long-suffering patience. Is this beyond the limits of what's possible?

I know that Mgr Lefebvre's disciples will object to my saying all this. They might say: 'You start off straightaway by putting right on your side. You start from the presupposition that the Council is sound from the point of view of Catholic doctrine and that the Mass of Paul VI is valid.' In dialogue, I would accept a discussion on this point, so long as my fellow-debaters did not exclude in advance a possibility which is actually the conviction of 2,500 bishops, 400,000 priests and hundreds of millions of the faithful.

MY BROTHERS – YOUR PLACE IN THE CHURCH

Your place is in the immense army of those who, doing their best, serve the Lord Jesus because he reigns, to the glory of God the Father. The world needs something other than our domestic bickering. My brothers, let us work together! Indeed, the rigour of your exigencies can benefit us. That the Theological Commission of the Council was able to carry out really quite notable work was in part due to a tenacious minority which kept forcing the Commission to be more precise – see, for example, the explanatory note preceding chapter III of *Lumen gentium*. You can play an analogous role in a reconciled Church – naturally, on the understanding that you do not come with a cantankerous, aggressive, or unintelligently intransigent spirit.

You often argue, from the fact that the Council was pastoral, that this proves that it was not doctrinal and that therefore it can be challenged. That argument doesn't stand up. It's true that one can discuss or throw light on one particular point or another, but a teaching of the Council does exist: to reject all of it, or even large parts of it, is tantamount to putting oneself in a dubious position in relation to the Catholic communion. Refusing to recognize the Mass of the Missal of Paul VI, together with other sacraments (e.g. Confirmation), as both valid and Catholic is equivalent to putting oneself outside this communion. I beg you to weigh up the consequences of a schismatic act. If you set up parishes or monasteries cut off from the main Church, you'd become something like the Old Catholics, or perhaps, more exactly, the 'Petite Eglise'* – except that your Church would have its clergy. You are convinced that you are upholding 'the Eternal Church'; but you can't be the Church opposed to the Church.[40]

* 'La Petite Eglise' – non-adherers to the Concordat of 1801 [Translator's Note].

These are Church questions of an exceptional gravity. The 29 August Mass at Lille leads one to ask a subsidiary question: what, or whom, are you playing around with? Who is it exactly who would take the risk of making use of you and thus blemishing your cause? I ask this question because I have heard it asked.

You want to celebrate Mass according to the Missal of St Pius V (modified on several points by other popes, his successors). You should be allowed the possibility of celebrating it in public, if it weren't for the fact that you give it an overtone of rejection – rejecting as non-catholic the Eucharist which we celebrate according to the Missal of Paul VI. The Missal, moreover, includes the Roman Canon and may be celebrated in Latin. The Mass of St Pius V is a sacred thing in itself, but to use it as an instrument of division and defiance is, from an objective point of view, a perversion of the Eucharist.

You have been strongly attacked. Many people are astonished, some even scandalized, that you should be harried tooth and nail while so many perpetrators of liturgical and theological irregularities are allowed to do their dirty work in peace. In his interview with M. Louis Salleron on 15 January 1976, Mgr Lefebvre noted that

'while authorized theological research is re-examining the very dogmas of our faith, I cannot understand how people can condemn me for discussing certain texts from a non-dogmatic Council. . . . For doing so I am being accused of infidelity to the Church, while none of these researching theologians is being condemned. There really are *two* different weights and two different sets of scales being applied.'[41]

I think that at least this much can be said: first of all, Mgr Lefebvre goes far beyond 'discussing certain texts from a non-dogmatic Council'. He acts as if he belonged to another Church (he would say: 'because the Pope and the entire episcopacy with their priests and the faithful belong to another Church – a liberal, democratic and modernist Church . . .') . . Next, he does occupy a certain position in the canonical and hierarchic system of the Catholic Church: he is much more get-at-able. Finally, alas, because of the turn that events have taken and because of what at the present time he is announcing as his future plans, one could be forgiven for thinking that a schism was in the course of being effected. Rome wants to stop him before he succeeds in establishing himself with his own ministers.

As far as the seminarians of Ecône are concerned, they are not the subject of any sanction, except those who have been odained in contravention of the provisions of Canon Law and who are accordingly subject to the censures – which have been a part of the Code since 1917 – that apply to those who do not observe these provisions. Unfortunately we are only able to deplore the fact that the application of these censures should have brought about some regrettable and painful situations, without being able to do anything at all about it.

The work of Ecône, as such, ought to be able to find its place in the Church, subject to the acceptance of the practical conditions of its communion – which is to say, in practice, the whole of Vatican II and the reforms which have followed it. *If* a truly regular seminary, similar to those that we knew, is able to form good priests, then God be praised! It certainly won't be the Pope or the competent Congregation who will be requesting its closure. *If*, on the other hand, it prepares priests in a schismatic perspective. . . .

My brothers, your place in the Church is with us, with our Pope Paul VI. We should be engaged in the fight for the faith, the celebration of the faith, together. Don't paint an adulterated picture of the Church that is faithful to Vatican II: she is still the Church of faith, love and mission. You would miss her – and she would miss you. It's up to you, then.

Mgr Lefebvre's 'Profession of Faith'

Rome, 21 November 1974

We adhere whole-heartedly, and with our whole soul, to Catholic Rome, Guardian of the Catholic Faith and of the traditions necessary to maintain that Faith, to Eternal Rome, Mistress of Wisdom and Truth.

On the other hand, we refuse and have always refused to follow the Rome of neo-modernist and neo-Protestant tendencies which clearly manifested themselves in the Second Vatican Council and after the Council in all the reforms which issued from it.

All these reforms, indeed, have contributed and are still contributing to the demolition of the Church, to the ruin of the priesthood, to the annihilation of the sacrifice and sacraments, to the disappearance of religious life, to a naturalistic and Teilhardian type of teaching in Universities, seminaries and catechesis, a teaching which is the fruit of liberalism and Protestantism and many times condemned by the solemn Magisterium of the Church.

No authority, not even the most elevated in the Hierarchy, can compel us to abandon or diminish our Catholic Faith, clearly expressed and professed by the Magisterium of the Church for nineteen centuries. 'If it should happen,' said St Paul, 'that anyone should teach you something different from what I have taught you, whether it be ourselves or an Angel from Heaven, let him be anathema' (Gal 1:8).

Isn't this what the Holy Father is telling us again today? And if a certain contradiction manifested itself in his words and in his acts, and similarly in the acts of the Dicasteries, then we would choose what has always been taught and would turn a deaf ear to the destructive novelities of the Church.

The *lex orandi* cannot be profoundly modified without also modifying the *lex credendi*. To the new Mass correspond a new Catechism, new priesthood, new seminaries, new Universities, a Charismatic Pentecostal Church – all things that are opposed to orthodoxy and the Magisterium as they have always been.

This reform, the fruit of liberalism and modernism, is completely and utterly poisoned; it starts from heresy and ends with heresy, even if not all its acts are formally heretical. It is accordingly impossible for any aware and faithful Catholic to adopt this reform and to submit to it in any way whatever.

For our salvation, the sole attitude of fidelity to the Church and to Catholic Doctrine is the categorical refusal of acceptance of the reform.

This is why, without any rebellion, bitterness or resentment, we are continuing our work of priestly formation under the Pole-Star of the Magisterium as it has always been, persuaded that we cannot render a greater service to the Holy Catholic Church, to the Sovereign Pontiff and to future generations.

This is why we formally hold to everything which has been believed and practised in the faith – the customs, worship, teaching of the Catechism, formation of priests, the institution of the Church – by the Church as she has always been and codified in the books which appeared prior to the modernist influence of the Council, while waiting for the true light of Tradition to dispel the shadows that darken the sky over Eternal Rome.

By this action, with the Grace of God and the help of

the Virgin Mary, St Joseph and St Pius X, we are convinced that we will remain faithful to the Catholic and Roman Church and to all the successors of Peter, and that we will be 'faithful dispensers of the Mysteries of Our Lord Jesus Christ in the Holy Spirit'. Amen.

Taken from *Itinéraires*, January 1975, as quoted by Jean Anzevui in *Le Drame d'Ecône. Analyse et Dossier*, pp. 88–9

APPENDIX II

Handwritten Letters from Paul VI

8 September 1975

Awareness of the mission that the Lord has confided to Us led Us on 29 June last to send you an exhortation, at once pressing and fraternal. Since this date We have each day been awaiting a sign on your part, expressing your submission – better than that: your attachment and your fidelity without reservation – to the Vicar of Christ. Nothing has yet come. It appears that you have not renounced a single one of your activities and that you are even formulating new plans.

Perhaps you are under the impression that your intentions are misunderstood? Perhaps you believe the Pope to be misinformed, or subject to pressures? Dear Brother, your attitude is so serious in our eyes that – We tell you again – We have Ourself carefully examined it, in all its constituent parts, with a prime care for the good of the Church and a particular attention to persons. It is after mature reflection and before the Lord that We have taken the decision which We confirmed to you in our previous letter.

It really is time that you declared yourself clearly. Despite the sorrow that it would cause Us to make public our interventions, We shall not be able to delay doing so any longer if you do not soon declare to Us your complete submission. For goodness sake, do not compel Us to take such a step, nor subsequently to penalize a refusal of obedience.

Pray to the Holy Spirit, Dear Brother. He will show you the renunciations that it is necessary to make and will help you to return to the path of full communion with the Church and with the successor of Peter. We invoke the same Spirit on you Ourself, while telling you once again of our affection and our tribulation.

> PAULUS PP. VI
> as quoted by Jean Anzevui's *Le Drame d'Ecône. Analyse et Dossier*, p. 115

To our revered brother Marcel Lefebvre

On this feast of the Assumption of the Most Holy Virgin Mary, we are eager to assure you that you are in our thoughts, and that this is accompanied by a special prayer for a positive and prompt solution of the question concerning your person and your activity with regard to the Holy Church.

These thoughts of you express themselves in the

following fraternal and paternal desire: that you would really consider, before the Lord and before the Church, in the silence and responsibility of your bishop's conscience, the insupportable irregularity of your present position. It does not conform with truth and justice. It arrogates the right to declare that our apostolic ministry is deviating from the rule of the faith and to judge as unacceptable the teaching of an ecumenical council held in accordance with the perfect observance of ecclesiastical norms. These are extremely grave accusations. Your position is not in accordance with the Gospel or the Faith.

To persist on this path would seriously damage your sacred person and those who follow you as a guide in disobedience to the Canon Laws. Instead of remedying the abuses which you want to correct, this would add another to them, and one of an incalculable gravity.

Have the humility, brother, and the courage to break the illogical chain which makes you a foreigner and hostile to the Church, that Church to which you have nevertheless given so much service and which you still desire to love and to edify. How many souls are waiting for this example of herosim and simply fidelity from you!

Invoking the Holy Spirit and entrusting to the Most Holy Virgin Mary this hour which is, for you and for us, a great and bitter one, we pray and hope.

'The Vatican makes a final appeal to Mgr Lefebvre', *Le Monde*, 29–30 August 1976

The Future of the Council

It is a month now since I started receiving letters and even visits in the desert asking me what I think about the Ecône drama. With a friendly insistence, Jean d'Ormesson urged me to write in *Le Figaro*. For a long time I preferred to keep silent. The problem posed by this affair is one of the most serious that can exist in the eyes of a philosopher of religion: I have not stopped thinking about it for half a century. As a Roman friend put it to me in a letter, to state my judgment in a sincere way has become for me 'a right and a duty'.

In a confused way, each one of us feels that, in the guise of a Latin Mass and a seminary, a question of prime importance is at stake, which affects the future of the Council.

Ecumenism has two faces, one radiant and full of hope, of a love which seeks to overcome the conflicts of Christians (as Leibnitz once wrote to Bossuet), the other pained and full of anguish, one which compels lofty consciences smitten with truth either to condemn on the one hand or to break away on the other. It is easy to express these dismemberings in terms of passionate emotion, ignorance or pride. In the final analysis, the reason Christians are divided is the conviction that they are being faithful to the will of Jesus Christ. All ecumenical ethics requires this reciprocal respect for final and divisive choices, as the most recent Council was at pains to emphasize.

I want to lift the problem as close to the light as possible, removed from any suspicion of polemic. I spent many years in close examination of the story of an illustrious convert, Cardinal Newman. This story throws a singular light on the Ecône drama. What does it tell us?

The Anglican Church, separated from Rome in the sixteenth century, had attempted an amalgamation of Protestantism and Catholicism. From 1837 until 1845, Newman was the leader of the Anglican High Church, which was drawing closer to Rome; but he reproached Rome for having 'corrupted' the Catholicism of the early centuries by adding new dogmas and new rites. In essence, this is the position of Ecône.

Newman was converted to Catholicism in 1845, and the reason he gave for his conversion was this: the Church, he said, must unite truth and life in herself. She must therefore change – rejuvenate herself, renew herself in order to maintain through change her fundamental identity: the acorn, to remain true to itself, becomes an oak-tree. In essence, this is the position of Vatican II. I might add, in passing, that I have often thought that a great council should be inspired by the thought of a single mind: Athanasius for Nicea, Thomas Aquinas for Trent; Vatican II was inspired by the thought of Newman.

Having recalled all this to mind, here is how I set out for myself the dual monologue of the bishop and the Pope.

Mgr Lefebvre considers himself as the defender of the faith. He reckons this faith to be compromised after ten years, not because it is assailed from without but because it appears to be unsure of itself and of its identity. People caricature the Bishop of Tulle and portray him as a belated lover of the past: what he thinks he is defending is the permanent faith of yesterday, today and tomorrow. At one time he restricted himself to saying that he accepted the Council but that he spurned certain consequences which had been improperly drawn from the Council. For some time now, and I cannot imagine why, he has acceded to a kind of logical vertigo: he claims that Vatican II was a schismatic council. This is an irrational aberration on his part.

As for Paul VI, he sees himself responsible in the eyes of history for the Council over which he presided, which he directed, which he brought to completion; and he demands of the bishop obedience to the successor of Peter, to the Vicar of Jesus Christ. Not that he believes himself to be infallible in his conduct, but because he has the supreme authority to have the Council put into effect.

Indeed, the Pope thinks that the Council opens up for the Church an immense source of hope at a decisive point in human history where the Catholic Church has the opportunity (so rare) to be respected and listened to by the world, and to appear as a factor of unity and salvation. The Council, according to the thought of Newman which is its inspiration, is developing the faith of ages under the impulse of the Spirit. It makes explicit certain characteristics ever present in the deposit of faith which in the course of past centuries had been implicit or obscured. Hence the freedom of conscience which is indispensable if faith is to be worthwhile, the common bases of monotheist religious and Christian confessions, etc. This is the spirit of that Paul whose name he chose, apostle of the Gentiles, making himself 'all things to all men' so that on the last day God may be 'all in all'.

Certainly Paul VI is in a better position than any other observer to weigh up the crisis of civilization, the crisis of the Church, and the acceleration of crises. He knows the decline of the spiritual life and of the faith. He knows of those liturgical extravagances which we keep quiet about, but which shake the confidence of the people and send the élite hurrying away on the tips of their toes. He has spoken with terror of the 'autodestruction' of the Church. . . . But confident in the Spirit, knowing that 'the gates of hell will not prevail', he hopes that after an inevitable crisis (the one which followed the Council of Nicea lasted for a century) the Church will get back to her cruising speed and be able to help humanity pass over a formidable threshold.

The Mass of Pius V is set up against the Mass of Paul VI, often in very abusive terms. Both pontiffs wanted to codify the most ancient traditions. The ritual of St Pius V established prayers which went back to the earliest centuries, as anyone will feel who reads these beautiful, simple texts. Paul VI simplified and enlarged. He proposed four 'canons' of which the first remains the former canon. The public was misinformed and disconcerted. How could one admit to the simple and the wise of this rational country that the only Mass celebrated by the Fathers of the Council would become the only one to be forbidden? How could one make the French, shaken out of their coherence and tolerance, understand that pluralism would respect all schools of thought, save that school which wants to retain the liturgy celebrated for so many centuries? In order to take root with the long, slow passage of time, a reform demands a process of maturing, indulgence and patience. It is time that our bishops reaffirmed the licitness of what Rome upholds without beating about the bush.

And one of the paradoxical results of so many paradoxes will be that the crisis will serve to accentuate the Holy See's power of arbitration in that it is the guarantor of the identity of the faith. Supremely responsible for the faith of yesterday, today and tomorrow, it is less influenced by public opinion than the bishops of an individual country.

Additionally, one has to envisage an almost fatal consequence. If the Roman See deals severely with Ecône, a visible target become a provocative one, logic will lead it to condemn even more those who, under the umbrella of the Council, are questioning the essence of the faith. Furthermore, in this period of reconciliation when Catholics are drawing closer to their brothers, they run the risk of finding themselves separated into three distinct families. Who wouldn't do everything possible to avoid that?

But what would happen if Ecône found itself, without admitting it, outside the communion of the Church tomorrow?

Well, the former Bishop of Dakar and Tulle would no longer be able to sit beside his brothers. He would find himself in the same position as the Archbishop of Canterbury. Then ecumenical honour would come into play, together with the recognition of wrongs done by both sides, the door still open to reconciliation, and the parable of the Prodigal Son. Mgr Lefebvre has always asked to be received alone and face to face by the Holy Father, like a son by his father. Once outside, the audience would be granted to him.*

It is impossible to escape from ecumenical love. Like all absolute love, ecumenism will always triumph: in joy as in sadness, as much in the communions which come together as in the separations which tear them apart. Will Christ be pulled to pieces right up to the end? And will he then find faith on the earth?

* This audience was in fact granted on 11 September 1976.

But ecumenical hope, which is a 'hoping against hope', knows that it will end in unity – in this world or in the next.

The Council, which defined openness, looks even more for fidelity. Shall I tell you what the joy of my faith is? It is, in receiving communion, to identify myself with the uncountable number of the faithful down twenty centuries . . .

All change supposes a permanence, and one still deeper than the change. (And this is true in politics, too.)

Alas! The worst is still possible; but we know that the best will one day come to pass. I used to love these words, so modest and so pure, which came from a friend who was an unbeliever: 'I know nothing. I have great difficulty in believing. I hope for everything.'

Jean Guitton of the Académie française
from *Le Figaro*, 27 August 1976

Action Française and Action Catholique: a brief explanation

The sermon delivered by Archbishop Lefebvre at Lille on August 29 came as a shock to many, in France and elsewhere.

Encouraged by the rather superficial coverage of the 'affair' undertaken by the mass media, many thought that Archbishop Lefebvre was the figurehead of a tendency within the Church which was reacting against certain liturgical and pastoral 'abuses' and that the conflict with the Vatican arose primarily on questions of form.

The political undertone of the sermon was probably what caused the most surprise. Any Frenchman who has studied a bit of history would not find much difficulty in identifying the nature of the more political views expressed by Archbishop Lefebvre: it is of a similar kind to the views upheld by the old movement Action Française. Significantly, some of its few remaining members were present at Lille.

Action Française was founded by Charles Maurras (1868–1952) in 1899. Maurras was a free-thinker who saw in Catholicism merely a 'religious habit' which, coupled with monarchical rule, it was necessary to maintain and encourage if France was to recover its old prosperity.

His doctrine was therefore anti-revolutionary, anti-parliamentary and nationalist, and as such it attracted a fraction of the French Catholics, both clergy and lay people. Conservative and 'integral' Catholicism (staunch traditionalists in France in the religious field are called *integristes*) also had, in common with Maurras' 'integral' nationalism, a marked hatred for the Jews, the Protestants and the International Socialists.

This fraction of Catholics hardened its position when, for the first time, the Vatican, in the person of Pope Leo XIII, preached reconciliation with the French Republic, thereby recognizing de facto the existence of modern democracy, fruit of the French Revolution.

The movement was condemned in a clumsy way by Pius XI in 1926, in terms more applicable to Maurras himself than to his followers. After a fairly strong resistance on the part of certain elements within the Church, the leaders of the movement finally submitted themselves to Rome in 1939.

Totally discredited for its part in the Second World War, the movement came to an end with the liberation of France. There remain, however, a fair number of people who belong to the same strongly-rooted extreme Right-wing current of thought which inspired Action Française.

During the same period, an increasing concern for social justice, and particularly for the condition of the working class, was being felt in another fraction of the French Church, often coupled with an interest in socialism. This period corresponded with the publication of the first great social encyclical of the Church, Leo XIII's *Rerum Novarum*.

Founded after the 1914–18 war, the Action Catholique movements provided the means by which this concern for social justice might be made effective, while in the intellectual sphere the movement 'Esprit' expressed the growing interest for socialism which was being felt by an increasing number of Christians.

The Second World War was a crucial period for the

development of the modern French Church.

While the Vichy régime appeared impregnated with Action Française ideology many Catholics were finding themselves fighting alongside Communists in the Resistance and were thereby discovering the huge gap which existed between official Catholicism and the working class.

The same can be said of the priests and seminarians who smuggled themselves among the workers who were being sent to labour camps in Germany. They realised how far Marxism, as a consequence of the total absence of Church presence and action in their midst, provided the only source of hope for the workers.

This explains the experience of the worker–priests after the war and the opening of the dialogue between Christians and Marxists.

More and more French Catholics found it necessary to give a concrete dimension to their Faith by joining Centre-Left or Left-wing parties, some even adhering to the practical aspects of Marxism.

A too-exclusive attention to the working-classes, a confusion on the part of a certain number of Catholics between what is specifically political and what is specifically religious, led some Catholics, particularly among the middle-classes, to follow Archbishop Lefebvre, until they realized that he was making exactly the same confusion from a Right-wing, and even extreme Right-wing, point of view (hence his references to the French Revolution and to Argentina).

Added to all this there is the undeniable dynamism of the Catholic Church in France, particularly since Vatican II, which has enabled a multitude of pastoral and also liturgical experiences to take place.

Francis Wilyte
reprinted from *The Catholic Herald*, London

Footnotes

1. Mgr Marcel Lefebvre, *Profession of Faith*, 21 November 1974. This is the text (reproduced in full in Appendix I) which caused the Holy See to act as it did.

2. These three quotations are taken from meetings of Mgr Lefebvre and published by him in *Un évêque parle* [A bishop speaks], pp. 196, 186 and 197 respectively. See also the letter to Paul VI of 17 July 1976 (text quoted above, p. 46). Similar but less developed terms are to be found in Mgr R. Graber's *Athanase et l'Eglise de notre temps* [Athanasius and the Church of our time], trans. A. Garreau, Paris 1973, pp. 34, 68, 74.

3. For further study on this point, useful reading is J. Labasse, *Hommes de droite, hommes de gauche* [Men of the Right, men of the Left], Paris 1947, chap. I: the issue numbered 7–8 of the *Chronique sociale de France* of 1956; M. Garrigou-Lagrange, 'Intégrisme et national-catholicisme' [Integrism and national-Catholicism] in *Esprit*, November 1959, pp. 515–43; J. Maître, 'Le catholicisme d'extrême-droite et la croisade antisubversive' [Extreme Right-Wing Catholicism and the anti-subversive crusade] in *Revue française de sociologie*, April–June 1961; also the books of E. Poulat.

4. Cf. Abbé Jean Anzevui, *Le drame d'Ecône* (Historique, analyse et documents) [The Ecône drama: history, analysis and documentation], Valprint, Sion 1976, pp. 13ff.

5. For example, writing in the review *Verbe* in 1957 and the years following, he favoured the setting up of *La Cité catholique*; he kept on pushing the idea of private property when at that time property in Africa was held in common. An article which appeared in *La France catholique* on 18 December 1959 under the title 'Les Etats chrétiens vont-ils livrer l'Afrique noire à l'Etoile?' [Are Christian States going to hand Black Africa over to the Red Star?] spoke against the movement towards independence and accused Islam (Senegal is 80% Muslim) of being the precursor of Communism. See J. B. Cisse, 'La longue poursuite d'un mirage intégriste' [The long pursuit of an integrist illusion] in *Afrique Nouvelle* no. 1415, 11–17 August 1976, pp. 12–16 and no. 1416, 18–24 August 1976, pp. 18–20.

6. Mgr Lefebvre was one of the active members of the *Coetus internationalis Patrum* which gathered together Council fathers of similar tendencies and on occasion organized concerted action, for example in the placing of amendments or in voting. He made several interventions to express his convictions, criticizing col-

legiality (11 October 1963, from a fairly pastoral point of view; 10 November, on the principle itself) and religious liberty (24 October 1964; 20 September 1965; also a petition for delay, 17–19 November 1964).

7. E.g. expressions like 'Protestant Mass' or 'Luther's Mass' for the reformed rites of the Eucharist. Insinuations that 'in the highest Roman circles there are *perhaps* persons who have lost the Faith' (*Un évêque parle*, p. 200) or that Mgr Bugnini is a Freemason. . . . If that were the case, would he have been made a Nuncio? This accusation, which was even extended to the Pope and a number of cardinals, was launched by the disgraceful newspaper *Il Borghese* and was taken up by Fr Bruckberger (in the newspaper *L'Aurore* on 8 July 1976); and this sort of tittle-tattle against Mgr Matagrin in *L'Aurore* provoked a lawsuit for defamation. A pretty unspeakable example of the disparaging association of ideas was that of the journal *Minute* (no. 750, 25–31 August 1976) which found itself unable to refer to the Abbé R. Laurentin without emphasising that he is the brother of Ménie Grégoire, who is known as 'Radio Sex' . . .

8. Baron Eckstein remarked long ago, about the Restoration: 'When a person says "freemason", "revolution", he is under the impression that he has paid his debt to healthy reason and explained the whole of history' (cf. *La Vie Intellectuelle*, 25 June 1936).

9. In a letter to Paul VI on 17 July 1976 (text published in *Le Monde*, 29–30 August 1976, p. 15), Mgr Lefebvre writes: 'If only Your Holiness would abandon this ill-fated undertaking of compromise with the ideas of modern Man, an undertaking which has its roots in a secret pact, which existed even before the Council, between high dignitaries in the Church and in Masonic Lodges.' That this belief is not peculiar to the Action Française but is typically conservative can be seen from Mgr R. Graber's pamphlet, mentioned above (footnote 2), *passim* and especially pp. 33–42.

10. Dom Guy Oury, *La Messe de saint Pie V à Paul VI* [The Mass from St Pius V to Paul VI], Solesmes 1976; Dom Paul Nau, *Le mystère du Corps et du Sang du Seigneur. La messe d'après saint Thomas d'Aquin, son rite d'après l'histoire* [The mystery of the Body and Blood of the Lord: the Mass as seen by St Thomas Aquinas, its rite as evidence by history], Solesmes 1976; A. Richard, *Le mystère de la Messe dans le nouvel Ordo* [The mystery of the Mass in the new Ordo Missae], Editions de l'Homme Nouveau, Paris 1970.

Since the drafting of our own book an excellent article by Mgr G. Martimort has appeared in *La Croix*, 26 August 1976.

11. Mgr Lefebvre during confirmations administered in the Salle Wagram on 4 October 1975 (*Pour l'honneur de l'Eglise* [For the honour of the Church], p. 20).

12. For the Thomist aspect, cf. P. Nau, *op. cit.*

On the traditional aspect, it is sufficient to quote St John Chrysostom, Doctor of the Church and father of the well-known liturgy: 'It is not a different sacrifice, but the same that we carry out today: or rather, we make a memorial of a sacrifice. [. . .] It is apparent that we do not offer a different sacrifice but simply accomplish the memorial of this unique and saving sacrifice' (*In Hebr. hom.*, 7, no. 3: PG 63, 131). And cf. the Council of Trent, Session XXII, Denz.-Schön. 1743, explaining Canon 3.

The opponents of the Mass of Paul VI argue persistently about no. 7 of the *Institutio Generalis* that appears at the beginning of the 1969 Missal. It has been admitted that this text, while in no way false, did not express clearly or completely enough what the Church is aware that she is doing in celebrating the Eucharist. This text was improved in the edition promulgated on 26 March 1970, and this is the one which is valid: there is nothing reproachable in it.

13. In 1953 I published a large book, *Jalons pour une théologie du laïcat* [*Lay People in the Church*] in which I based my treatment of the lay exercise of the classical functions of priest, king and prophet on the distinction between these functions as an exercising of baptismal dignity and as a 'hierarchic' office or 'power'.

14. I gathered a lot of evidence on this point in one of my two contributions to the volume *La liturgie après Vatican II* [The liturgy after Vatican II], 'Unam Sanctam' series, 66, Paris 1967, pp.241–82.

15. We have discussed schism and heresy in a section about break-ups of unity in *L'Eglise une, sainte, catholique et apostolique* [The Church: one, holy, catholic and apostolic], 'Mysterium salutis' series, 15, Cerf, Paris 1970, pp. 65ff.

16. *De Catholicae Ecclesiae unitate*, c. 17.

17. *Commentary on the 'Summa'*, 2a 2ae, q. 39, a.1.

18. Additionally, the Abbé Denis Roch in his sermon on 4 July 1976 during a Mass celebrated in Geneva by a newly-ordained priest said: 'Who knows if Ecône is not a little David, trusting in God, who has the task of overthrowing a Goliath trusting in Man – a Goliath who has penetrated into the Church in order to convert the world by human means?'

Chapter 2

19. I provided copious documentation, both in *Lay People in the Church*, especially chapter V, and in 'Quod omnes ab omnibus tractari et approbari debet' in *Rev. hist. Droit fr. et étranger*, 1

958 part 2, pp. 210–59.

20. The best explanations are those of J. Ratzinger (chap. V, pp. 101ff, expanding an article dating from 1965, in *Le nouveau peuple de Dieu* [The new people of God], Paris 1971); G. Philips (*L'Eglise et son mystère au Deuxième Concile de Vatican* [The Church and her mystery at the Second Vatican Council], Desclée 1967, vol. I, pp. 277ff.); H. de Lubac (*Les Eglises particulières dans l'Eglise universelle* [Particular Churches within the universal Church], Paris 1971). For the historical aspect, see among others J. Lécuyer, *Etudes sur la collégialité épiscopale* [Studies in episcopal collegiality], Le Puy and Lyon 1964; and Y. Congar, *Ministères et communion ecclésiale* [Ministries and ecclesial communion], Paris 1971, pp. 95ff.

21. *De Catholicae Ecclesiae unitate*, c.5.

22. The integrists have outrageously abused a phrase, admittedly ill-judged, which I used when writing about the voting on the College at the Council, 30 October 1963: 'The Church has undergone, peacefully, her October Revolution' (*Le Concile au jour le jour* [*Report from Rome*], Second Session, p. 215). They twisted this into a confirmation of the Sovietization of the Church! It was simply a writer's image not a very good nor very fortunate one. To make anything else of it is to give it a meaning which it never had and which I categorically do not accept.

23. Mgr Lefebvre in *Lettre aux amis et bienfaiteurs* [Letter to friends and benefactors], no. 7, 1 October 1974, cited by Anzevui, *op. cit.*, p. 59.

24. *L'Aurore*, 22 January 1976.

25. J. Courtney Murray, 'Vers une intelligence du développement de la doctrine de l'Eglise sur la liberté religieuse' [Towards an understanding of the development of the Church's doctrine on religious liberty], in *Vatican II. La liberté religieuse*, 'Unam sanctam' series, 60, Paris 1967, pp. 111–47. The illuminating intervention of Cardinal Journet can be read in *Doc. cath.*, 1965, coll. 1799–1800, which concluded 'The actual Declaration in my opinion deserves full approval'.

26. All three published by Fayard, 1960 and 1963. We would at least draw attention to the one most accessible to the general public: *La Tradition et la vie de l'Eglise* [Tradition and the life of the Church], in the 'Je sais – je crois' collection, only 130 pages long.

Chapter 3

27. In *Athanase et l'Eglise de notre temps* (cf. footnote 2), p. 68.

28. *Le Pape du Ghetto* [The Ghetto Pope], p. 82.

29. An example of generalization: 'Ten years after its [the Council's] closure, what is there that remains of our liturgy but

rags and tatters? What is there that remains of our theology but an infamous stew of Marxism, Freudism, science and sociology? [. . .] What is there left of our preaching but a puerile demagogy that would discourage even a veteran parliamentary radical socialist?' (Fr Bruckberger in *L'Aurore*, 8 January 1976). Is this serious? No. I could just as easily quote a similar passage in J. M. Paupert's paper 'Nous sommes des misérables' [What wretched creatures we are], published in *Le Monde*, 1 September 1976.

30. D.-P. Auvray, 'Où va la messe?' [Where is the Mass going to?] in *Carrefour*, 14 July 1976, p. 4.

31. *Apologia I to Antonine the Pious*, 67, 5.

32. L. Bouyer, 'L'improvisation liturgique dans l'Eglise ancienne' [Liturgical improvisation in the early Church] in *La Maison-Dieu* no. 111 (1972-3), pp. 7–19. The whole of this number is devoted to 'creativity and liturgy'.

33. I am sorry not to talk about it at all, but I really have no competence to do so. But I often get complaints. One correspondent writes: 'Furthermore, catechesis has been criticized, for example by Cardinal Daniélou (*Pourquoi l'Eglise*? [Why the Church?], p. 64), Mgr Elchinger (*La liberté d'un évêque* [The freedom of a bishop], pp. 144–72) and the Sovereign Pontiff himself (Allocution to the Sacred Consistory, 24 May 1976: *Doc. cath.* no. 1700, 20 June 1976, p. 558) who also asked for a solid, precise, easily-memorable catechetical basis (*Doc. cath.* no. 1676, 18 May 1975, p. 454). Was he therefore implying that our present catechesis does not evidence these qualities?'

34. For example, Abbé J. Kamp's book *Credo sans foi et Foi sans credo* [Belief without faith and Faith without belief], 1974, was severely criticized by Cardinal Suenens (cf. *Doc. cath.* no. 1669, 2 February 1975, pp. 143–4) and we also discussed it in *Rev. Sciences phil. et théol.*, 59 (1975), p. 213. But see also the discussion held with the author by the Louvain professors in *Rev. théol. de Louvain*, 6 (1975), pp. 267–72 and 388–401. There was also very active, and even more radical, discussion of books by Hans Küng.

35. However, the allegation seems to me to be ambiguous, for it can mean 'complete with all the actually-existing disorders and injustices', or 'without toppling the government or the constitution, but still promoting the necessary reforms', or it can have other meanings again. Nevertheless, I will maintain that 'it's the system, the order of things, which must be re-examined in order to really effect the reforms which justice demands . . .'.

36. Cf. Amos 2:6ff. and 8:5–6; Isaiah 1:17 and 58:3–12. Compare with James 1:20; 2:1–9; 4:13–5:6.

37. I refer to Paul VI's letter *Quadragesima adveniens* of 14 May

1971 (*Doc. cath.* no. 1587, 6 June 1971, pp. 502–13) which it is essential to re-read carefully; I refer also to *Lourdes* 1972. *Politique, Eglise et Foi* [Politics, Church and Faith], Centurion, Paris 1972. I mention additionally my own *Ministères et communion ecclésiale* (cf. footnote 20), pp. 229–59 (on 'unity and pluralism') and *Un peuple messianique. Salut et libération* [A Messianic people: salvation and liberation], Paris 1975.

Pour une Eglise partisane is the title of a book by my confrére Alain Durand, who criticizes the Lourdes 1972 text.

38. See, for example, Jacques Tessier, 'Une très grand question', *La Croix*, 18 August 1976, against a sort of monopoly exercised by the 'Marxist option' movements.

Chapter 4

39. John XXIII's sermon in the course of his enthronement ceremony in the Cathedral of St John Lateran, 23 November 1958. *Doc. cath.*, 21 October 1958, coll. 1605–4. Fr H.-M. Féret, who quotes this text ('La théologie concrète et historique et son importance pastorale présente' [Concrete and historical theology and its present pastoral importance] in *Le service théologique dans l'Eglise* [Theological service in the Church], Cerf, Paris 1974, pp. 193–247), also quotes a speech of 27 November 1958 on the occasion of the opening of the university year at the Lateran Seminary: 'Reading the Book, the great Divine Book . . . exalted by prayerful voices over the Christian centuries . . . is not a question of a simple contemplation of religious truth or of a truth bound up with theological or philosophical doctrine but also of deductions and practical directives for the apostolate of souls . . .' (*ibid.*, coll. 1624–5).

40. The example occasionally cited of St Athanasius does not prove the point. First of all it is necessary to take St Jerome's words about a world that would wake up to find itself Arian with a pinch of salt. There were faithful bishops and faithful laity, as Newman showed. The popes, except for poor Liberius for a a very short space of time, supported Athanasius. But if, even so, the example of *one* faithful bishop could be formally invoked, the present situation of the Church is totally different from what it was in the years 325–62. Malpractices exist in the Church, and we have mentioned them; but where are the heretical bishops? Where are the prevaricating councils or conventicles? There is room for an imitation of Athanasius' faith and courage. But there is no parallel situation.

41. This interview makes up document no. 23 of J. Anzevui's *Le drame d'Econe*; the passage quoted occurs on p. 132.